MANAGING PEOPLE

Managing Universities and Colleges:
Guides to Good Practice

Series editors:

David Warner, Principal and Chief Executive, Swansea
Institute of Higher Education

David Palfreyman, Bursar and Fellow, New College, Oxford

This series has been commissioned in order to provide a systematic
analysis of the major areas of the management of colleges and
universities, emphasizing good practice.

Current and forthcoming titles include:
Frank Albrighton and Julia Thomas (eds): *Managing External Relations*
Allan Bolton: *Managing the Academic Unit*
Robert W. Bushaway: *Managing Research*
Ann Edworthy: *Managing Stress*
Judith Elkin and Derek Law (eds): *Managing Information*
John M. Gledhill: *Managing Students*
Alison Hall: *Managing People*
Christine Humfrey: *Managing International Students*
Colleen Liston: *Managing Quality and Standards*
Patricia Partington and Caroline Stainton: *Managing Staff Development*
Harold Thomas: *Managing Financial Resources*
David Warner and David Palfreyman (eds): *Managing Crisis*
David Watson: *Managing Strategy*

MANAGING PEOPLE

Alison Hall

Open University Press

Open University Press
McGraw-Hill Education
McGraw-Hill House
Shoppenhangers Road
Maidenhead
Berkshire
England
SL6 2QL

email: enquiries@openup.co.uk
world wide web: www.openup.co.uk

First Published 2003
Copyright © Alison Hall 2003

A catalogue record of this book is available from the British Library

ISBN 0 335 20993 9 (pb)   0 335 20994 7 (hb)

Library of Congress Cataloging-in-Publication Data
CIP data has been applied for

Typeset by RefineCatch Limited, Bungay, Suffolk
Printed in the UK by Bell & Bain Ltd, Glasgow

To Dave and Anna. Your support made this book possible.

CONTENTS

3   Managing the early days   `50`

SERIES EDITORS' INTRODUCTION

∎

Post-secondary educational institutions can be viewed from a variety of different perspectives. For most of the students and staff who work in them they are centres of learning and teaching in which the participants are there by choice and consequently, by and large, work very hard. Research has always been important in some higher education institutions, but in recent years this emphasis has grown, and what for many was a great pleasure and, indeed, a treat, is becoming more of a threat and an insatiable performance indicator, which just has to be met. Maintaining the correct balance between quality research and learning/teaching, while the unit of resource, at best, holds steady, is one of the key issues facing us all. Educational institutions as workplaces must be positive and not negative environments.

From another aspect, post-secondary educational institutions are clearly communities, functioning to all intents and purposes like small towns and internally requiring and providing a similar range of services, while also having very specialist needs. From yet another, they are seen as external suppliers of services to industry, commerce and the professions. These 'customers' receive, *inter alia*: a continuing flow of well qualified, fresh graduates with transferable skills; part-time and short course study opportunities through which to develop existing employees; consultancy services to solve problems and help expand business; and research and development support to create new breakthroughs. It is an unwise UK educational institution which ignores this aspect, which is now given a very high priority by the UK government.

However, educational institutions are also significant businesses in their own right. One recent study shows that higher education institutions alone are worth £35 billion a year to the UK economy.

Moreover, they create more than 562,000 full-time equivalent jobs either through direct employment or 'knock-on' effects. This is equivalent to 2.7 per cent of the UK workforce. In addition, it has recently been realized that UK higher education is a major export industry with the added benefit of long-term financial and political returns. If the UK further education sector is also added to this equation, then the economic impact of post-secondary education is of truly startling proportions.

Whatever perspective you take, it is obvious that educational institutions require managing and, consequently, this series has been produced to facilitate that end. The editors have striven to identify authors who are distinguished practitioners in their own right and, indeed, who can also write. The authors have been given the challenge of producing essentially practical handbooks, which combine appropriate theory and contextual material with many examples of good practice and guidance.

The topics chosen are of key importance to educational management and stand at the forefront of current debate. Some of these topics have never been covered in depth before and all of them are equally applicable to further as well as higher education. The editors are firmly of the belief that the UK distinction between these sectors will continue to blur and will be replaced, as in many other countries, by a continuum where the management issues are entirely common.

Since the mid-1980s, both of the editors have been involved with a management development programme for senior staff from higher education institutions throughout the world. Every year the participants quickly learn that we share the same problems and that similar solutions are normally applicable. Political and cultural differences may on occasion be important, but are often no more than an overlying veneer. Hence, this series will be of considerable relevance and value to post-secondary educational managers in many countries.

It is a truism to say that further and higher education is a 'people business'. On average, institutions spend 58 per cent of their turnover on staff, although within this figure there are considerable variations, some institutions spending as much as 70 per cent. Staff are not only by far the highest cost element for a further or higher education institution, they are also its most complex area of activity. The lay person might assume that almost all further and higher education employees are 'dons' – that is, teachers and researchers. Not so. In reality, well over half of permanent higher education staff are employed as secretaries, clerical staff, administrators (or should that be 'managers'?), technicians, librarians, computer experts, manual workers and a host of other specialist categories. The erroneous lay view is reinforced by the fact that we do not even have a general term to describe all of these employees, relying instead on the appalling negative 'non-academic staff', although in some higher education institutions, some of these staff have risen to the heights of being known as 'academic-related'.

At the moment, despite growing evidence to the contrary, we are still working within a culture in further and higher education where most employees think that they have 'a job for life' when a permanent post has been gained. The structure of *Managing People*, therefore, is particularly apposite because the author has employed a chronological sequence from recruitment through to parting company. Alternatively, each chapter can be read as a self-contained guide to a particular aspect of managing people.

Alison Hall has not only produced a comprehensive and user-friendly handbook, but also one which is replete with valuable templates and checklists. For instance, there is particularly helpful guidance on induction, interviewing and disciplinary issues. *Managing People* achieves an excellent balance between such supportive advice and scholarly referencing. Indeed, one of the series editors was so taken by the draft manuscript that he smuggled a copy to his personnel colleagues before publication. Such reprehensible action speaks for itself!

David Warner
David Palfreyman

ACKNOWLEDGEMENTS

I am grateful to Jo Daley for permission to reproduce the induction checklist used at Sheffield Hallam University and to Jonathan Bursey for permission to reproduce the University of Bath's *Code on Academic Freedom and Corresponding Responsibilities*. I am also grateful to Sue Wheeler and Diane Thomason at the University of Leicester for their assistance with aspects of Chapter 5.

LIST OF ABBREVIATIONS

ACAS   Advisory Conciliation and Arbitration Service
AUT   Association of University Teachers
BBSRC   Biotechnology and Biological Sciences Research Council
CEML   Council for Excellence in Management and Leadership
CIPD   Chartered Institute of Personnel and Development
CNAA   Council for National Academic Awards
COSHH   Control of Substances Harmful to Health
CRB   Criminal Records Bureau
CRS   contract research staff
CUCO   Commission on University Career Opportunity
DDA   Disability Discrimination Act
EAT   Employment Appeals Tribunal
EFQM   European Foundation for Quality Management
EWC   expected week of childbirth
FEO   Flexible Employment Options
FETO   Fair Employment and Treatment Order
FHEA   Further and Higher Education Act
GOC   genuine occupational qualification
GP   general practitioner
HE   higher education
HEFCE   Higher Education Funding Council for England
HEI   higher education institution
HR   human resource(s)
HSE   Health and Safety Executive
ILTHE   Institute of Learning and Teaching in Higher Education
MRC   Medical Research Council
NEBS   National Examining Board for Supervision and
        Management

Ofsted	Office for Standards in Education
OJT	on the job training
Pilon	pay in lieu of notice
PR	public relations
RCI	Research Careers Initiative
ROA	Rehabilitation of Offenders Act
RRA	Race Relations Act
SDA	Sex Discrimination Act
SOSR	some other substantial reason
TUC	Trades Union Congress
UGC	Universities Grants Committee

SETTING THE SCENE

Introduction

The need to manage people is much the same in any large organization. They must be recruited, developed, motivated, rewarded and, regrettably, sometimes disciplined and dismissed. However, the way in which people are managed varies enormously from one organization to another. Some organizations (although fewer than there were) are paternalistic, having a relatively high regard for the well-being of the workforce, while giving staff little opportunity to influence policy or practice. Others are aggressively goal-oriented, requiring staff to 'shape up or ship out'. Still others are heavily bureaucratic, where every aspect of the employment relationship is governed by rules, regulations and procedures. The management of people in a university or college is influenced by the organization's culture and history just as much as anywhere else, so a brief look at the historical origins of higher education institutions (HEIs) might be helpful.

Until the early nineteenth century, just two small universities – Oxford and Cambridge, both of which arose in the late twelfth/early thirteenth centuries – served England.[1] The universities of Durham and London were chartered in the 1830s, but it was from the mid-nineteenth century that the pressure increased for an expansion in, and evolution of, higher education (HE) provision. There was growing criticism of the 'monastic ideal' of Oxford and Cambridge, which was felt to be irrelevant to the needs of modern, industrialized society.[2] The first university colleges were founded in the latter part of the nineteenth century (in Manchester, Newcastle, Birmingham, Bristol, Leeds, Nottingham, Sheffield and Liverpool), preparing students for

University of London examinations. By 1957, there were a total of 21 universities in Great Britain.

From the latter years of the nineteenth century, government took a growing interest in HE – a reflection of the increasingly important position that it held in the economy as a result of a growth in student numbers and the development of significant industrial and scientific research in the universities. This interest found expression in the formation of the Universities Grants Committee (UGC) in 1919. The government, through the UGC, pursued a policy of expansion from 1945, and in 1961 the Robbins Committee was appointed to recommend ways in which further expansion might be achieved. One recommendation was the promotion of the colleges of advanced technology (Bath, Brunel, City, Heriot-Watt, Loughborough, Salford, Strathclyde and Surrey) to university status.[3] Another was by breaking the university monopoly on degree-awarding powers – the creation of the Council for National Academic Awards (CNAA) allowed polytechnics to offer degree-bearing courses. Thus, the binary system came into being, with government funded universities on the one hand and local authority funded polytechnics on the other. The binary system came to an end (supposedly) in 1992, when the polytechnics (and three colleges of HE) were granted university status and freed from local government control by the Further and Higher Education Act (FHEA).

The role of the visitor in pre-1992 universities

The papacy was instrumental in supporting the early medieval universities. There was papal support also for the teachers and scholars at approved universities, who could then remain resident at the university while enjoying the income from some distant parish. However, by far the most important aspect of papal blessing for a university was its designation as a privileged corporation, set apart from the citizens of the town in which it was located, and enjoying very distinctive legal protection. The teachers and scholars were not subject to secular jurisdiction, but could be tried only in ecclesiastical courts. The charter of privileges awarded to Oxford University in 1214 even included a clause requiring the burgesses of the town to swear to maintain the clerical immunity of the scholars from arrest by the lay authorities.[4]

The office of visitor originated from the bishops' desire to ensure the proper governance of the universities in their respective dioceses and the bishops of Lincoln and Ely exercised their right of visitation on Oxford and Cambridge throughout the thirteenth and fourteenth centuries. From the latter years of the seventeenth century, the courts generally took the view that the visitor of an eleemosynary corporation (that is, a charitable foundation established for a particular purpose) had sole jurisdiction to oversee the internal management of that corporation and to determine complaints from corporation members regarding the internal management. As charitable foundations for the promotion of learning, the colleges of the ancient English universities are eleemosynary corporations and subject to the jurisdiction of the visitor. (However, the *universities* of Oxford and Cambridge themselves are civil corporations, as they were created for other than charitable purposes.) All other pre-1992 universities are eleemosynary corporations, as they have been founded for educational purposes and the traditional role has been transferred to the visitors of these institutions.[5] However, the House of Lords' decision in the case of *Thomas* v. *Bradford* (1987)[6] led to a fundamental change to the visitor's powers in relation to employment matters. In this case a lecturer's contract of employment was terminated as a result of her persistent refusal to comply with her head of department's instructions. The dismissal had the effect of ending her membership of the university. Thomas complained that in dismissing her, the university had failed to follow its own procedures as set out in its statutes. The university argued that the substance of Thomas' complaint was within the visitor's exclusive jurisdiction. The House of Lords agreed and noted that in exercising their proper authority, the visitor is a court whose decisions may only be overturned by a superior court on the grounds of errors in jurisdiction, defects in procedure or points of law, but not by way of appeal on a question of fact. As a result of this judgement, s206 of the Education Reform Act 1988 removed the exclusive jurisdiction of the visitor in relation to any dispute relating to the appointment or employment of a member of the academic staff, or the termination of such employment.

When the post-1992 universities were created by the FHEA, their governing bodies were established as civil corporations and are therefore subject to civil jurisdiction, so they have no visitor.

The suspicion of 'management' ◼

The medieval universities of Oxford and Cambridge were organized on 'magisterial' lines. That is, the masters' guild directed the university's affairs – selecting new masters, regulating the masters' duties and determining the academic regime. It was the 'effective hub of university government'.[7] By the end of the fifteenth century, the division between academic and administrative roles had not yet appeared and in addition to their academic duties the masters also discharged administrative functions. Day-to-day control of the university was in the hands of an elected vice-chancellor (the chancellor usually being an absent dignitary). The chief executive and financial officers were the proctors, who were also elected by and from the teaching body. The proctors supervised the timetable, organized university ceremonies, enforced discipline and assisted the vice-chancellor in the transaction of business between the university and the town. Teaching staff also performed other roles such as acting as principals of halls and colleges, deputizing for the chancellor or vice-chancellor to hear minor cases in the chancellor's court, effecting repairs to university property, collecting rents, and so on. With the rapid expansion of HE in the first half of the twentieth century, the administrative role of the academic did not disappear, but changed in character. As universities grew into relatively large, complex organizations dependent on a variety of sources of income, professional administrators emerged and assumed responsibility for many aspects of university management, beginning with financial administration and estates maintenance, but all important decisions (and a great many trivial ones) were taken by committees of academics.

In the pre-1992 universities, academics still hold most of the influential management positions (head of department, dean and pro-vice-chancellor), often on a rotating basis. This, perhaps, is one reason why 'management' has not really been taken seriously until relatively recently – managing (a department, a faculty, a function) was something to be fitted in alongside the 'proper' job of being an academic – that is, to engage in research and to teach. The situation in the post-1992 universities is quite different. Having their roots in local government, they are used to being 'managed' rather than administered. The positions of pro-vice-chancellor (and also, often, dean and head of department) are open-ended managerial posts, filled by competitive recruitment. The post-holders are senior managers, with significant line management responsibility, who largely eschew their erstwhile academic lives.

Another reason why 'management' has been (and, to a variable extent, still is) viewed with suspicion in HE is the high proportion of the workforce made up of highly qualified knowledge workers – the academics. Academics tend to conform in almost every respect to Raelin's definition of a 'cosmopolitan professional'.[8] Such professionals generally have only a marginal loyalty to the organization in which they work, preferring to align themselves with their peers within their discipline for the purposes of recognition and evaluation. As employees, they demand high levels of autonomy and participation in their work and resent close supervision, particularly by a 'manager'. Indeed, the management of academic staff has been likened to 'herding cats'![9] Although a survey of universities in northern England by MacKay[10] suggested that 'The traditional arms-length relationship regarding academic staff is losing ground to a distinctly managerial approach in which academics are viewed as resources making a contribution to the realization of the institution's goals', the *ideal* of the individual, independent scholar is still strongly held, particularly in pre-1992 universities.

Yet the need for effective management has outstripped not only the development of the structures but also of the people that would deliver it. Universities and colleges are large, complex organizations, the largest employing thousands of staff and with a turnover in multi-millions. Every academic is expected to be a manager – of resources, of people, of money – without having been selected on the basis of their management aptitude and often with little access to management development once in post. That's where this book comes in. It has been written with the academic-as-manager in mind (although the content is equally relevant to a manager who is not also an academic), and assumes no prior training in human resource (HR) management. It takes the reader logically through the stages in the employment relationship – how to recruit the right person into the right job, how to develop, motivate and reward them, how to approach the work-life balance, how to deal with issues such as discipline and ill health and, finally, how to end the relationship fairly and, hopefully, with as little acrimony as possible.

How this book can be used ▮

Although the book follows a chronological sequence, from recruitment through to parting company, each chapter is a self-contained guide to an aspect of the management of people – reading the book from cover to cover is not necessary, although readers with little experience of recruiting staff and managing them in their early days would benefit from reading the first two chapters together. More experienced managers may wish to 'dip in' for advice on specific topics. The summaries at the end of this section give an overview of the scope of each of the chapters in the book.

During the late 1960s/early 1970s one major high street bank ran a television advertising campaign that featured a bank manager sitting at an imposing desk, in a wardrobe. The idea was that customers of this bank had access to professional, financial advice whenever and wherever they needed it. This book will, hopefully, perform the role of the personnel/HR professional on the bookshelf, available for consultation at any hour of the day or night. It will certainly provide answers to many questions that line managers think are too trivial to trouble someone in personnel/HR about (but which, in reality, are actually quite important). *But*, no book can substitute for the support of experienced professionals who use their local knowledge of the institution and its culture to tailor their advice to a particular situation. This book is intended to supplement, not replace, the support of these professionals and, at various points throughout the book, readers are advised to consult the personnel/HR department in their own institution.

The book has been written as a practical guide and, as there are many situations that individual managers in HE will come across only infrequently (for example, long-term sickness, drug/alcohol abuse or a complaint of harassment), the various processes are set out in detail. Wherever possible, specific points are illustrated by examples from case law or case studies.

Chapter summaries

Chapter 2: Managing to get the right person for the job

This chapter provides a comprehensive overview of the recruitment and selection process, from writing the job description and person specification, to breaking the good (and the bad) news. Practical advice is set in the legal context, and the appendix includes examples of job descriptions, person specifications, adverts and a 'starter set' of interview questions.

Chapter 3: Managing the early days

This chapter looks at the processes you need to think about when planning for the arrival of a new member of staff – induction, probation and training. It explains the importance of an effective induction programme and provides advice to mentors and probationary supervisors appointed to support new members of staff. A model probationary monitoring scheme is suggested, and the appendix includes an example of an induction checklist.

Chapter 4: Managing for performance – today and tomorrow

Robin Middlehurst and Tom Kennie examine managing for performance in HE. They describe the international, regional and national context, before reviewing the theoretical basis for performance management. Finally, they look at the techniques of performance management in practice and include practical advice on giving feedback and measuring performance.

Chapter 5: Managing tricky situations

It would not be surprising if many readers skipped the early chapters in the book and went straight to this one! This chapter provides practical advice, set in an appropriate legal context, for handling a range of tricky situations: sickness (both long-term and short-term, but recurrent), disability arising during the course of employment, drug/alcohol problems, mental health problems, stress, discipline, grievances, harassment and bullying.

Chapter 6: Managing work-life balance

Catherine Simm explains in a clear and straightforward way the statutory background to maternity, paternity, adoption and parental leave and then goes on to address the pros and cons of a variety of flexible working arrangements. Using a combination of examples from case law and case studies, she demonstrates that work-life balance initiatives can benefit both the institution and the member of staff.

Chapter 7: Managing the termination of employment

All employment relationships come to an end. In the majority of cases, the parting of the ways between an employer and employee is entirely straightforward. However, this isn't always the case. This chapter sets out the legal basis for ending the employment relationship and, using examples from case law, illustrates the concepts of unfair and constructive dismissal. It looks briefly at tenure, the Model Statute and academic freedom and gives advice on how to handle a dismissal fairly in a range of circumstances. Finally, some advice is provided on how to handle resignations and employment references.

And finally . . . a cautionary note ■

It is inevitable that any book concerned with the management of people will be rich in legal references – less than a dozen major statutes relevant to personnel were enacted in the 100 years to 1970, but in the three and a bit decades since then, more than 30 major pieces of relevant domestic legislation have been passed. Given the rate at which employment law changes, both in the UK and in Europe, it is likely that, even by the time this book appears, the review of legislation included in it will no longer be comprehensive.

2

MANAGING TO GET THE RIGHT
PERSON FOR THE JOB

Introduction

It is worth investing time and effort in getting the recruitment and
selection process right. The process itself is costly, both in terms of
money and staff time, while the consequences of making a poor
appointment can have a deleterious impact on the effectiveness of the
whole department. Succeeding in matching the right person to the
right job isn't a guarantee that the employment relationship will be
trouble-free, but failing to do so almost invariably leads to problems
later on.

The selection process isn't just about ensuring that the right person
is appointed, from the recruiter's point of view, it also allows the candidate to find out more about the job, the department and the institution (and therefore be in a better position to judge whether the job is
right for them). It is also an excellent opportunity for the institution
to promote a positive image to the outside world.

The flow chart in Figure 2.1 will help recruitment novices to maximize their chances of success.

Organizations differ in the extent to which their personnel professionals are involved in the recruitment process, some having
devolved most of the activity to departments, while others take a
more centralized approach. Whatever the pattern in your organization, your personnel/HR department will be able to advise on every
step of the recruitment and selection process, both generally and with
regard to local policies and practices.

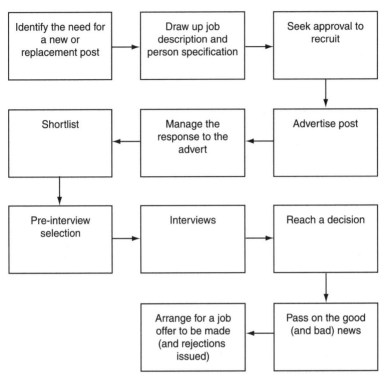

Figure 2.1 A flow chart of the recruitment and selection process (adapted from a flow chart in Loughborough University's Good Recruitment Guide)

Legal considerations

The discrimination legislation

Various pieces of legislation apply to employers in Great Britain which prohibit discrimination on the grounds of race, colour, nationality, ethnic origins, sex, marital status and disability. These are outlined briefly below. It is also illegal to discriminate on the basis of sexual orientation (from 2003) and religion (from 2006). Separate legislation applies to employers in Northern Ireland and this is noted in the relevant sections.

Sex Discrimination Act (SDA) 1975 and the Race Relations Act (RRA) 1976

Under the SDA it is unlawful to discriminate against someone on the basis of their sex or marital status. Certain parts of the Act are written in terms of discrimination against women but its provisions apply equally to men. Under the RRA it is unlawful to discriminate against a person on racial grounds, that is, on the basis of their colour, race, nationality or national or ethnic origins.

In relation to employment, it is unlawful for employers in Great Britain to discriminate against job applicants or existing employees because of their sex or marital status or on racial grounds by:

- denying them job interviews;
- refusing them access to employment;
- offering them less favourable terms and conditions of employment;
- withholding opportunities for promotion, training or transfer;
- dismissing them or subjecting them to other less favourable treatment.

Similar provisions applying to employers in Northern Ireland are found in the Race Relations (Northern Ireland) Order 1997 and the Sex Discrimination (Northern Ireland) Order 1976 (amended 1988).

Persons who believe that they have been unfairly discriminated against on any of the prohibited grounds may complain to an employment tribunal. If the complaint is upheld, compensation awards are likely to be substantial and there is no upper limit on the amount of compensation that may be awarded. It is also unlawful to treat less favourably someone who has brought discrimination proceedings, or who has given evidence or information in connection with such proceedings.

The legislation applies to all employers, regardless of size and also applies to self-employed workers and subcontractors.

Both the sex and race discrimination legislation include the concepts of direct and indirect discrimination. Direct discrimination is quite straightforward. For example, an employer who refuses to employ a person because they are black would be guilty of direct discrimination. Similarly, an employer who refuses to employ a woman because she is pregnant is guilty of direct sex discrimination. Indirect discrimination, however, is more subtle. It is when a condition or requirement is imposed, even unintentionally, which cannot be objectively justified, with which a considerably smaller proportion of women (or men), or members of a particular racial group can comply, and which results in a detriment to the person who cannot comply with it. It is no longer necessary for the condition or requirement to be something that must be complied with. A claim could still succeed if it could be shown that the condition was preferred, desirable or discretionary. Box 2.1 includes some examples of indirect discrimination.

Box 2.1   Indirect discrimination – some examples

Example 1[1]

Mrs B was employed as a cleaner with an additional quality control function, beginning work at 8 a.m. After several years in post, she was told that she had to start work at 7 a.m. She said she could not do this because of family commitments (Mrs B could not begin work before 8 a.m. because she had to see that her children got up and were ready for school). She eventually agreed to relinquish her quality control work and to work solely as a cleaner so that she could continue to start work at 8 a.m., but initiated a grievance about the loss of the quality control job. This was not resolved to her satisfaction and she resigned, claiming constructive dismissal. The tribunal found that the requirement to begin at 7 a.m. indirectly discriminated against women and that the reasons given by Mrs B's former employers to justify the requirement to start at 7 a.m. rather than 8 a.m. were not convincing.

Example 2[2]

A temporary postal worker of Asian origin was required to take an aptitude test before being given a permanent contract. She failed the test and complained of indirect racial discrimination. She was successful – the Post Office test figures showed that Asian employees were less likely to pass than other racial groups.

Example 3[3]

Applicants for certain cleaning positions were required to complete a 15-minute, 20-question written test in English. Three applicants, all of Asian origin, failed the test and complained of indirect discrimination. The tribunal found that the written test in English was such that the proportion of the applicants' racial group that could comply with the requirement was much smaller than the proportion of persons not of that racial group. The tribunal also found that the use of the test could not be justified by the requirements of the job.

Example 4[4]

Ms A applied for the post of language coordinator with a city council's ethnic minority language service. One of the selection criteria
was the possession of a professional qualification in teaching, youth
work, social work or community work. Ms A did not possess such a
qualification and was not shortlisted. She claimed that she had
been indirectly discriminated against. The tribunal defined the pool
of potential applicants for the post as 'that section of the community in Britain who has completed their secondary education by
passing "A" levels, who have since gained experience in adult
education working with members of ethnic minorities and who are
proficient in at least one ethnic minority language'. It found that
the professional qualification requirement was one with which a
considerably smaller proportion of people of Asian origin could
comply with than compared to people of non-Asian origin. The
tribunal also found that the council could not show that the
requirement was objectively justifiable. It found that a professional
qualification was not needed to do the job, but was being used by
the selection panel as evidence of an organized mind and disciplined way of thinking. The tribunal found that this justification
did not outweigh the discriminatory effect of the requirement.

There are a few, very limited, circumstances where it is permitted to
discriminate on the basis of sex or race, known as genuine occupational qualifications (GOCs). These are limited to situations such as
dramatic performances or artistic and photographic modelling when,
for reasons of authenticity, a person from a particular sex or racial
group is required, and to jobs where the holder will be performing
personal welfare services which are most effectively provided by a
member of that racial group or, for reasons of decency, by a man or a
woman.

Both Acts permit positive action in limited circumstances to redress
gender or racial imbalances. An organization is permitted to encourage applications from a particular sex or racial group (for example,
through targeted advertising) where few or no members of that sex or
racial group have been undertaking the work in question in the pre-
ceding 12 months. However, it must be remembered that it is illegal to
directly discriminate in favour of someone on the basis of their sex,
race or nationality.

Race Relations (Amendment) Act 2000

The Race Relations (Amendment) Act 2000 requires public bodies, including universities and colleges, to eliminate racial discrimination, promote equality of opportunity and promote good relations between people of different racial groups. Specifically, universities and colleges are required to prepare a written policy on race equality, to assess the impact of that policy on ethnic minority students and staff and to monitor the recruitment and progress of ethnic minority students and staff.

Equal Pay Act 1970 (amended 1983)

The Equal Pay Act is intended to eliminate discrimination in the pay and conditions of women and men undertaking:

- like work;
- work of equal value;
- work rated as equivalent.

'Pay' includes salary, sick pay, shift allowances, bonuses and so on. The Act does not require that men and women in comparable posts should be paid identically, but that any significant differences should be based on objectively justified factors unrelated to sex.

Although the Act only protects against unequal pay between men and women, advice to employers is to ensure that pay structures are equitable for people from different racial groups and for people with and without disabilities.

In Northern Ireland, the Equal Pay Act (NI) 1970 (amended 1984) applies.

Disability Discrimination Act (DDA) 1995 and the Special Educational Needs Discrimination Act 2000

The DDA 1995 is intended to eliminate unfair discrimination against people with disabilities. The idea is that a person's disability should not be a bar to employment unless it would significantly interfere with their ability to do the job, and there are no adjustments that the employer could be reasonably expected to make (to the working environment, the way the work is done, to hours of work and so on).

A disabled person under the Act is anyone 'with a physical or mental impairment which has a substantial and long-term adverse effect on his [sic] ability to carry out normal day-to-day activities'.

The employment provisions of the Disability Discrimination Act have been in force since 1996. There are two main ways in which an employer might discriminate against a disabled person:

• By treating them less favourably (without justification) than other employees or job applicants because of their disability. Some examples of justified and unjustified unfavourable treatment are given in Box 2.2.

Box 2.2 Justified and unjustified unfavourable treatment – examples

Example 1[5]

Ms F had undergone treatment for a depressive illness for six years. She was offered the post of residential social worker by a local authority, subject to a medical assessment. The employment offer was withdrawn four months later because Ms F had not obtained satisfactory medical clearance. The tribunal found that the authority had made an assumption, without good reason, that Ms F would require a lot of sick leave and had taken no account of a reference that had contradicted this assumption or of the fact that she had been in good health for the previous 18 months. The tribunal decided that Ms F had been subjected to unjustified unfavourable treatment because of her disability.

Example 2[6]

Mr T, an epileptic, was successfully interviewed for a job as a baggage handler at Heathrow Airport and was asked to undergo a medical examination by the employers' occupational physician. The physician noted in her report that baggage handlers are required to drive 'airside' and that Mr T failed to meet the medical standards set by the Driver and Vehicle Licensing Agency for driving in this situation. He also failed to meet the medical requirements for work at unguarded heights, work in fuel tanks or in confined spaces or work on moving machinery – all situations that a baggage handler may encounter in the course of their work. As a result of the physician's report, Mr T was informed that he had been unsuccessful in his application. The tribunal found that Mr T had suffered less favourable treatment as a result of his disability but that it had been justified because safety was of paramount importance in airside operations and that none of the reasonable adjustments that the employer could have made would have enabled him to carry out the work of a baggage handler safely.

Box 2.3   Reasonable adjustments – examples

Example 1[7]

Mr M worked as a service engineer with British Gas. His employers were unaware that he was an epileptic until he blacked out at work while driving. The employers insisted that he should not return to work until his general practitioner (GP) had confirmed in writing that he was fit to do so. They then offered him a transfer to a clerical position which was lower paid and, unlike his previous position, did not provide the opportunity to work overtime. The tribunal found that the employer had failed to make reasonable adjustments.

Example 2[8]

Ms K was an architect working with a local authority. She went off sick with tennis elbow. Her employers arranged a workplace assessment and, as a result, offered her the option of returning to work on a trial basis using a modified workstation, a dictaphone and a hands-free telephone. Although Ms K declined the offer and was eventually dismissed, the employers were found to have complied with the duty to make reasonable adjustments.

- By refusing to make reasonable adjustments (without justification). A variety of factors must be taken into account in determining whether an adjustment is reasonable (including the expected benefit from making the adjustment, the degree of disruption involved in making it, the resources of the employer and so on). Some examples are given in Box 2.3 to illustrate when it may or may not be reasonable to make an adjustment.

Schedule 8 of the Act set out modifications that apply to its application in Northern Ireland.

Rehabilitation of Offenders Act (ROA) 1974

It is inevitable that many job applicants will have a criminal record, as a third of all males will have been convicted of a criminal offence by the age of 30, along with 8 per cent of all females.[9] The intention of the ROA is to protect those convicted of minor offences from discrimination in employment. Minor offences (those which carry a non-custodial sentence, or a period of custody not exceeding 30 months) are 'spent' after a period of time known as the 'rehabilitation period'. Rehabilitation periods vary depending on the sentence imposed for the conviction, whether any other offences have subsequently been committed and the period of time that has elapsed since the conviction. Table 2.1 illustrates the rehabilitation periods for a range of sentences.

There are certain convictions which are never spent, including:

- a sentence of imprisonment for life;
- a sentence of imprisonment, or equivalent detention for young persons, exceeding 30 months;
- a sentence of preventative detention.

Table 2.1 Rehabilitation periods specified by the ROA

Sentence	Rehabilitation period
Imprisonment (or equivalent detention for young persons) for more than 6 months but not more than 30 months	10 years[1]
Cashiering, discharge with ignominy or dismissal with disgrace from Her Majesty's service	10 years[1]
Imprisonment (or equivalent detention for young persons) for not more than 6 months	7 years[1]
Dismissal from Her Majesty's service	7 years[1]
Detention is respect of a conviction in service disciplinary proceedings	5 years[1]
A fine or any other sentence not covered by the ROA	5 years[1]
Probation	5 years from date of conviction[2]
Conditional discharge or binding over	1 year or until order expires
Absolute discharge	6 months
Disqualification (for example, from driving)	Period of disqualification
Hospital order with or without a restriction order	5 years, or a period ending 2 years after order expires (whichever is the longer)

[1] May be reduced by half for person under 18 at the date of conviction.
[2] In the case of someone under 18 at the date of conviction, 2½ years from the date of conviction or a period beginning with the date of conviction and ending when the order ceases.

Once a conviction is 'spent' a rehabilitated person does not have to disclose its existence. Also, an employer cannot refuse employment (or dismiss an existing employee) on the basis that the person has a spent conviction. A number of occupations are exempted from the ROA but only a few are potentially relevant to universities and colleges. These are listed in Box 2.4. Applicants for, or existing employees in, exempted employment are required to disclose 'spent' convictions.

Where the employment involves working with children or vulnerable adults, employers are required to apply for disclosure of convictions from the Criminal Records Bureau (CRB). There are three types of disclosure that the CRB can provide:

- *Basic*, which provides details of a person's unspent convictions.
- *Standard*, which provides details of all current and spent convictions, cautions, reprimands and final warnings. This type of disclosure is appropriate to employment which may involve contact with children or vulnerable adults and to employment in positions of trust (for example, in the legal and accountancy professions). An example relevant in the HE sector would be that of a reader employed to support a student with a visual impairment.
- *Enhanced*, which includes all the information in the standard disclosure, plus checks on local police records. It may also include other information – for example, on current investigations – which must not be disclosed to the applicant. This type of disclosure is appropriate to employment that involves a greater degree of contact with children or vulnerable adults such as teaching and day care. An example relevant to HE might be that of a researcher employed to interview children on a one-to-one basis or a nursery nurse employed in a university nursery.

Box 2.4 Employment exempted from the ROA which may be relevant to universities and colleges

- Employment involving regular contact with children or vulnerable adults
- Medical practitioner
- Dentist, dental hygienist, dental auxillary
- Veterinary surgeon
- Nurse, midwife (and certain employment concerned with the provision of health services)
- Ophthalmic optician, dispensing optician
- Pharmaceutical chemist

Both the standard and enhanced disclosures include checks against lists maintained by the Department of Health of persons judged to be unsuitable to work with children or vulnerable adults.

Organizations wishing to apply for disclosures must register with the CRB and abide by its code of practice. Recruiting managers who believe that it would be appropriate to seek disclosure in respect of applicants for a particular post should, therefore, contact their personnel or HR department for advice as early in the recruitment process as possible.

The Fair Employment and Treatment (Northern Ireland) Order (FETO) 1998

FETO only applies in Northern Ireland. It makes it unlawful to discriminate against someone on the grounds of religious belief or political opinion. The definitions of direct and indirect discrimination used by FETO use the same construction as used in the sex and race legislation in Great Britain. FETO places a number of duties on employers. These include:

- *Registration*: all private sector employers with more than ten employees working more than 16 hours per week must register with the Equality Commission for Northern Ireland (certain public sector employers are automatically deemed to be registered).
- *Monitoring*: registered employers must submit an annual return to the Equality Commission giving details of the community background of their workforce.
- *Article 55 reviews*: all registered employers must review their recruitment, training and promotion practices at least once every three years.

Fixed-term Employees (Prevention of Less Favourable Treatment) Regulations 2002

The regulations, which came into force on 1 October 2002, implemented the European Union directive on fixed-term work. They ensure that fixed-term employees are treated no less favourably than employees doing the same work who are employed on an open-ended basis. 'Less favourable treatment' is not limited to terms and conditions of employment, but applies to any aspect of employment, including training, appraisal and study leave. The regulations limit successive fixed-term contracts to a maximum of four years.[10] This means that the employer is obliged to convert a fixed-term contract to a permanent one after four years unless an objective justification for the employment continuing on a fixed-term basis can be demonstrated. The limit on a fixed-term contract does not apply to first contracts, so that if someone is offered a five-year contract, the four-year rule does not come into effect unless the contract is renewed.

Part-time Workers (Prevention of Less Favourable Treatment) Regulations 2000

These regulations implemented the European Union directive on part-time work and ensure that part-time workers receive no less favourable treatment with regard to their terms and conditions of employment than someone undertaking the same work on a full-time basis, in the absence of an objective justification. This means that part-time workers are entitled to the same hourly rate of pay, access to occupational pension schemes, holiday entitlement, occupational sick pay and access to training and so on, as a full-time worker in the same job.

Data Protection Act 1998

The Data Protection Act 1998 governs the collection, storage and use of personal data, in any format (paper, electronic, tape, microfilm and so on). 'Personal data' means any information that relates to an identifiable individual and includes names, addresses, date of birth, salary and other financial information, medical details and so on. Personal data must be:

- kept securely;
- held for no longer than is necessary;
- used for the purpose(s) for which it was collected;
- not disclosed to any unauthorized person, either orally or in writing, accidentally or otherwise;
- accurate and, where necessary, kept up to date.

Individuals are entitled to ask to see the data that an organization holds about them. Part 1 of the Employment Practices Data Protection Code, published in March 2002, which covers recruitment and selection, stipulates that applicants will normally be entitled to have access to interview notes about them that are retained as part of the interview records. Also, while confidential references are exempt from disclosure by the organization that gives them, this exemption does not apply once the reference is in the hands of the organization that requested it. However, the recipient is entitled to withhold information that reveals the identity of other individuals, such as the identity of the author of a reference.

The Asylum and Immigration Act 1996

Under Section 8 of the Asylum and Immigration Act 1996, it is a criminal offence to employ a person who is subject to immigration controls unless the person has current and valid permission to be in the UK and that permission does not prevent them from taking the job in question. Citizens of the European Economic Area (that is, countries of the European Union plus Iceland, Liechtenstein and Norway), Switzerland and some other groups (listed in the Appendix to this chapter), are not subject to immigration controls and are free to live and work in the UK.

In most cases, a work permit will be required to employ an overseas national who is subject to immigration control. Work permits are issued for the employment of a named individual in a specific job for a limited period of time and are not transferable. The personnel/HR department is normally responsible for applying for a work permit, rather than staff in the recruiting department. The provision of immigration advice and services (which could include issuing a letter of invitation to enable an overseas national to apply for a visa to enter the UK) is strictly controlled by the office of the Immigration Services Commissioner and only designated individuals in a university or college are authorized to provide them.

Recruitment

Job descriptions

It isn't just good practice to start the recruitment process by formulating a job description, it will markedly reduce the risk of making an unhappy appointment. The process of identifying the key duties and responsibilities of a job will help you to see the post in relation to others in the team (as it is and as it needs to be) and discourage preconceived notions (such as, 'this is what we want because this is what we've always had'). For example, in relation to a research post, don't just describe the overall project, think about the new researcher's role in it, how much supervision they will need (and, as importantly, how much you or others will be able to provide) and whether they will be

---

Box 2.5   Job descriptions

The following information should normally be included in a job description:

- *Job purpose:* to accurately reflect what the job is about.
- *Duties:* this shouldn't be just a list of tasks but should reflect the objectives of the job. This section should be specific (avoid vague terms such as 'clerical work') but not overly prescriptive – room should be left for flexibility and growth. Don't overemphasize what will, in reality, be relatively minor tasks – the job description should be an accurate reflection of what the job will involve.
- *Special conditions:* this section should identify any aspect that would be considered unusual; for example, if it involves shift work or is for a temporary period only.
- *Organizational responsibility:* who the post-holder is responsible to and the number and seniority of staff they are responsible for.

---

responsible for supervising others. If you are recruiting a member of secretarial staff, you may want to consider whether the vacancy presents an opportunity to reorganize the secretarial support in your section or department, thereby providing development opportunities for existing staff. Box 2.5 gives more details about the kind of information that should appear in a job description.

Person specifications

Once you have produced a job description, you can begin to think about the attributes that the person who will ultimately fill the position will need, in terms of experience, skills and abilities, qualifications and so on. When compiling the person specification, refer to the job description – you need to identify the attributes that will be required to carry out those duties and responsibilities to a satisfactory standard, not list every desirable attribute that would come in useful! The person specification, setting out essential and desirable attributes, will provide the selection criteria for the post, so what is included must be relevant and justifiable in terms of the ability to perform the duties of the job. It is also important when compiling the person specification to consider how you will measure the applicants against the criteria. For example, if you decide that the professor you are recruiting must have the ability to provide academic leadership in their discipline, what measures will you use to judge this? Similarly, if

you decide that your new secretary must be a good team player, how will you decide whether the person sitting opposite you is one of the Three Musketeers or a latter-day Greta Garbo? See Box 2.6 for more details about the kind of information that should appear in a person specification.

Some examples of job descriptions and person specifications in different formats are given in the Appendix to this chapter.

Box 2.6   Person specifications

The person specification should normally include the following:

- *Experience:* this is the experience that a person must have before they can do the job (essential) and the experience that would allow them to do it more effectively (desirable). For example, for a research post, experience of a particular technique may be essential, while previous experience of applying that technique in a particular context may be desirable. For a secretarial post, previous secretarial experience may be essential, while that experience gained in an education setting may be desirable. It is generally unhelpful to specify an arbitrary number of years experience as essential – it is the quality and relevance of the experience rather than the quantity that is important. Similarly, age should not be used as a criterion. Age discrimination, illegal in the UK from 2006, may be indirectly discriminatory if it has the effect of making it more difficult for certain groups (women, certain racial groups or people with disabilities) to meet the requirements of the job (see also pages 10–11).
- *Skills and abilities:* these are the practical skills and abilities necessary to do the job. For example, an administrator for a research project would need the organizational skills to file project and financial reports appropriately, both electronically and in paper-based systems; a research assistant working on a project involving face-to-face interviews with people whose first language is not English might need to speak one or more relevant languages.
- *Qualifications:* these are the minimum educational or vocational qualifications that are required, and any that might be desirable. For example, for a lecturing post, you may decide that a good first degree in a relevant subject is essential, but that a doctorate is merely desirable. For senior financial posts, you may require the post-holder to have a recognized professional qualification, but not necessarily demand that they be a graduate.
- *Training:* include here any practical training that the post-holder will be required to undertake.

- *Other:* this is the section in which to include attributes that are necessary to do the job, but that don't fit readily into any of the categories above. For example, you may decide that a new lecturer should be enthusiastic or that a new researcher should demonstrate initiative. This section, in particular, should be used with care. Requiring a new recruit to have a sense of humour might seem a good idea, but humour is determined, in part, by both culture and gender, and there is a risk of unfair discrimination if it is used as a selection criterion (not to mention the practical difficulties of measuring it).

Advertising

Once you have a job description and person specification, you have the tools to write an advert. However, it's a good idea to pause for a moment at this point and consider the reasons for advertising. The most obvious, of course, is to attract people to apply for the post, without having to rely on word of mouth recruitment, which has the potential for unfair discrimination. There are other reasons for advertising, however, which include:

- to produce a reasonable field of suitable applicants;
- to enhance the image of the organization (be it the department, faculty or the institution as a whole);
- to comply with agreements that the institution may have with recognized trade unions;
- to comply with organizational recruitment policies.

Where an advertisement is placed depends on:

- the nature of the post (for example, advertising in the local press is still probably the most effective way of reaching potential applicants for most secretarial and manual jobs, but for research posts internet advertising alone can be successful);
- the funds available to support recruitment (press advertising, particularly in specialist journals, can be expensive, whereas advertising via subject-specific websites is often free, but won't necessarily have the same impact);
- organizational recruitment policies (including any policies with the aim of increasing the number of job applicants from certain groups including ethnic minority communities, women/men or people with disabilities).

> **Box 2.7** Advertising media
>
> - *National press,* including the minority press (for academic, research and senior administrative posts where the target labour market is national or international)
> - *Local press* (for support posts, where the target labour market is locally-based)
> - *International and national specialist journals* (for academic and certain research and specialist administrative posts)
> - *Internet* (for all posts, but particularly useful for research posts)
> - *Networks* (subject networks are useful for research posts, networks for minority communities are useful for ensuring the widest possible coverage)
> - *Recruitment agencies* (expensive, but can be useful for very senior or hard to fill specialist posts)

Box 2.7 sets out the most-used advertising media for recruitment. TV and radio advertising is expensive, and would normally only be considered for large-scale recruitment exercises, or as part of the organization's wider public relations (PR) strategy.

In addition to being legal, decent, honest and truthful, a successful advert should also be clear, logical, relevant and concise. It should attract (and maintain) interest, give accurate information about the job and the organization and include instructions for potential applicants on how to apply. Use the job description and person specification as the basis for the advert and ensure that the language used won't deter under-represented groups (for example, advertise for a 'security officer' not a 'security man' or for 'waiting staff' rather than 'waitresses'). Although adverts in the free media can be somewhat longer, resist the temptation to throw in the kitchen sink – people are less likely to apply for a post if they've lost interest in the advert halfway through. Remember that you will have an opportunity to give more details in the further particulars (see below). Box 2.8 gives more details about the kind of information that should appear in an advert, and some examples are given in the Appendix at the end of the chapter.

Further particulars

Providing applicants with further particulars allows you to give more information about the job, the department and the institution than is

---

Box 2.8   Recruitment advert contents

- Use the job description to produce a clear and informative summary of the main duties of the job
- Use the person specification to describe the essential and desirable skills, experience, qualifications and qualities that applicants should possess
- Include details of salary and any special employment conditions (for example, contract duration if the post is temporary or the necessity for shift work if applicable)
- The offered salary should be realistic – don't advertise an inflated figure to attract interest if there is no possibility of someone being offered the post at that level
- Include details of the application procedure (how to obtain an application form, to whom completed forms should be returned and the closing date)
- Complete a final equal opportunities 'health check' to ensure that the advert complies with legal and good practice requirements

---

feasible in an advert. It is helpful to potential applicants if the job description and person specification are included and it ensures that all enquirers receive the same information. The nature and volume of the extra information will depend to a large extent on the type of post being advertised. For example, the further particulars for an academic post would normally include a list of the undergraduate and postgraduate programmes offered by the department and a description of its research groups; for a technical post supporting teaching, the further particulars may include a description of the number and type of laboratory classes supported, while a copy of the project proposal may be included in the further particulars for a research post. Remember that the legal provisions applying to adverts also apply to the supporting information, so a final equal opportunities health check should be carried out before the information is circulated.

Managing the response to the advert

As mentioned previously, it is important that all potential applicants receive the same information about the advertised post and one way to ensure this is to make up applicant packs (with an application form, job description, person specification and any further details), preferably *before* the post is advertised. Application forms are preferable to CVs as they:

- streamline the shortlisting process because all the relevant information is presented in the same format;
- can be more helpful to selectors than a CV, which highlight those aspects of the application that the candidate had chosen, not the selector;
- ensure that certain information essential to the organization is collected early in the recruitment process.

For some posts (for example, academic and research posts) it may be necessary to specify that certain information, such as a publications list or research strategy, is included with the completed application form, but it is advisable to discourage applicants from including a complete CV.

Increasing numbers of organizations are now able to provide further particulars and an application form electronically and this can reduce both the cost and time involved in the recruitment process. However, adequate time should be allowed to permit potential applicants who do not have access to email or the internet to obtain and return a completed application before the closing date.

If a named individual is given as a contact in the advertisement, care should be taken to ensure that any contact with potential or actual applicants is limited to providing factual information about the job and the organization. The process should not be used to gather information about potential applicants in an informal way or to encourage or deter potential applicants.

It is good practice to acknowledge all applications, but this can be done by asking applicants to provide a stamped addressed postcard for the purpose, or alternatively via email, if you are confident that confidentiality will not be breached.

Selection ∎

Shortlisting

This is the process whereby applicants are matched to the essential and desirable characteristics specified in the job description. It is good practice for shortlisting to be carried out by a minimum of two people and the same selectors should consider all the applications, to ensure consistency. Shortlisting should be undertaken as soon as possible after the closing date. A helpful way to approach shortlisting is to use

Applicant reference number	1	2	3	4	5	6	7	8	9
Essential									
Previous secretarial/clerical experience									
Previous experience in a 'customer-facing' role									
Experience of working in a large organization									
Audio-typing skills									
RSA II or equivalent in typing or word processing									
Desirable									
Previous experience of working in HE									
Familiarity with Microsoft Office software									
Study or qualifications in office practice									

Figure 2.2 Example of a shortlisting matrix for a clerical post

a matrix, similar to the one shown in Figure 2.2. It encourages object-ivity and readily indicates those candidates that meet the person specification and those that do not.

It is important to remain objective and to follow the criteria derived from the person specification. Don't make assumptions about the abilities of different sexes, or of applicants with disabilities. For example, if a job requires heavy lifting such as moving barrels in a cellar, it should not be assumed that an applicant would not be physically capable of carrying out the task simply because she is female. Similarly, it should not be assumed at the shortlisting stage that an applicant would be unable to successfully work in a customer-facing role just because they had a physical or sensory disability. It is particularly important not to make assumptions about the ability of disabled applicants to undertake some or all of the duties of the post, as employers are legally obliged to make reason-able adjustments to enable an otherwise qualified disabled person to carry out the job.

Popular posts that attract large numbers of applicants can perturb inexperienced selectors – they can be so overwhelmed that they become obsessed with looking for ways to reduce the numbers. The rules in this situation are simple:

- Don't impose an arbitrary limit on the shortlist.
- Don't introduce additional criteria that are irrelevant to the needs of the post. For example, one employer was found guilty of indirect racial discrimination because it used the application form as a test of abilities which were not necessary to do the job in question (such a test, if irrelevant to the job, may also unfairly discriminate against applicants with certain disabilities). Another was found guilty of indirect racial discrimination when it excluded applicants with addresses containing a particular postcode – the action excluded a significantly higher proportion of non-white applicants than white applicants.
- Use the 'desirable' criteria to reduce the numbers.
- If necessary, 'weight' the value of 'desirable' criteria to reduce the numbers still further, but ensure that any weighting is applied to all applicants who satisfy the essential criteria.

If there have been few applicants for a post, don't be tempted to shortlist any applicants who fail to meet the essential criteria to 'make up the numbers'. Interviewing unsuitable applicants is not a good use of anyone's time and reflects badly on the organization.

A checklist for shortlisting is provided in Box 2.9.

Box 2.9   Shortlisting checklist

- Use the job description and person specification
- Consider using a matrix
- Check each applicant against the essential criteria
- Check facts against criteria, where possible (for example, qualifications)
- Don't use guesswork to eliminate applicants
- Guard against making assumptions about the abilities of groups of people in general, that may not be true of individuals
- Don't impose arbitrary limits (upper or lower) on the shortlist
- Don't introduce irrelevant criteria to reduce numbers

Practical testing (including presentations)

Despite the relatively low success rate of the traditional unstructured interview as a means of predicting the best person for a job[11] it is still the selection method of choice in HE, for the majority of jobs. By and large, recruiting managers just wouldn't feel comfortable offering a job to someone they hadn't interviewed. However, the careful use of testing will add to the usefulness of the interview.

For academic posts, it is common for shortlisted candidates to be invited to present a seminar to members of the department, usually on their current teaching or research interests. You should decide in advance what the purpose of the presentation is. Is it designed to give an idea of how a candidate might handle teaching or their grasp of, and ability to answer questions on, their research area? The task set for the candidates may well be different depending on the purpose. However, whatever the task, all candidates, including internal ones, should be invited to give a seminar. If comments from those attending the seminar are to be fed back to the interview panel, this should be made clear to the candidates in advance and a standard feedback form issued to attendees.

For secretarial and clerical posts it is not uncommon for a word processing test to be used (the near ubiquity of Microsoft Word nowadays means that problems posed by unfamiliarity with particular software are reduced). Testing in technical recruitment is less common, but a task that could be set for an electronics technician might include building simple electronic components.

It is important when designing tests as part of the selection process to consider whether the proposed task is:

- useful (that is, will it actually give you information about the candidates' abilities that you wouldn't otherwise have access to);
- relevant (that is, does the task form part of the regular duties of the post);
- fair (that is, will all the candidates be able to complete the task regardless of disability).

A task that is useful and relevant may still be unfair. If this is the case, try to adapt the task, or find a suitable alternative.

Assessment centres

An assessment centre is essentially a varied suite of selection techniques, carried out on a group of candidates over one or more days. The concept has not been greatly used in HE, even for the most senior posts, although it could be argued that it lends itself to the diversity of skills required in the modern university or college. The assessment centre may include individual and/or group exercises (including problem solving), group discussions, psychometric tests, presentations and interviews. Assessment centres are costly to set up and run, but can be useful if well designed and there are many good candidates to choose from. A good assessment centre, closely linked to the job description and person specification, with thoughtful feedback to all candidates, will capitalize on the enthusiasm of successful candidates and leave even those who are rejected with a favourable impression of the organization.

Headhunting

The use of search consultants in HE in the UK has tended to be limited to the most senior and/or specialized management and administrative roles (for example, vice-chancellors, registrars, directors of finance, heads of marketing and publicity, and so on). Consultants don't come cheap and it is vital that an organization not only does its homework properly to select a company with an appropriate track record, but also has a clear (and clearly articulated) job description and person specification for the post.

Headhunting conducted on a less formal basis goes on all the time, however, although the people doing it might not always recognize it as such. The investigator who emails a colleague and asks if they know of anyone who might be interested in their new grant is headhunting. So too is the vice-chancellor who asks an external assessor for a professorial appointment for suggestions of who might be invited to apply. Such activities must be handled carefully, even when the post is advertised as well, and all applicants, however they came to hear about the post, must be treated equally, as applicants who have been 'invited to apply' may feel more confident and perform better as a result.

Use of references

For employment purposes, the most useful references are from a candidate's current and former employers. The most detailed information is likely to be supplied by line managers, but there are some organizations that insist that all references are provided by the HR department. In these cases, the information provided is likely to be limited to the dates of employment, job title, salary on leaving and other 'technical' details. There is little value in taking up personal references as such referees are invariably complimentary.

Organizations differ in their practice regarding the timing of taking up references. Some take up references on shortlisted candidates prior to interview, others take up references only when an appointment has been offered. In the former case, it is important to check that the candidate does not object to their current employer being contacted (serious embarrassment, or worse, could result if the employer is unaware that the individual is considering leaving). In the latter case, the position should be offered 'subject to satisfactory references being received', as it will not be possible to withdraw an offer, or to dismiss an employee, because of an unsatisfactory reference if such a condition is not explicitly included in the contract. For example, in the case of *Stapp* v. *The London Borough of Hillingdon*,[12] Mr S was offered a job, subject to satisfactory references. The offer was withdrawn when the reference turned out to be unsatisfactory although the letter informing Mr S of this did not arrive until after he had left home to start his new job. The tribunal found that, as the condition included in the offer had not been fulfilled, the contract had not come into existence. On the other hand, in the case of *Faris* v. *Red Cross*,[13] the tribunal found that the contract was valid because the condition regarding satisfactory references was not included in the offer letter, but a subsequent one sent after Ms F had accepted the job.

Ask referees from the current or most recent employment to confirm details such as length of service, job title, attendance, reason for leaving and so on. Although the Chartered Institute of Personnel and Development (CIPD) does not recommend asking referees to comment on the candidate's suitability for the post they have applied for, it is perfectly proper to ask a referee to give examples from their experience of the candidate to illustrate the ways in which they match the job description and person specification. You should provide referees with a copy of the job description and further particulars so that they are able to provide informed and relevant comments. Invite written references (transmitted by fax if there is limited time) as these are likely to be fuller and more considered. Although telephone references can be faster (and sometimes more revealing), experienced interviewers should take them and full notes should be made. Email references risk breaching the Data Protection Act 1998, as it is not possible to guarantee confidentiality unless a secure link is used, and should, therefore, be avoided.

Part 1 of the Employment Practices Data Protection Code states that a confidential reference is exempt from disclosure to the subject of the reference by the organization which gave it, but the exemption does not apply to the recipient. However, the recipient is entitled to withhold information that might identify the author of the reference.

Two different styles of reference requests are shown in Box 2.10.

Box 2.10   Reference requests – two different styles

Example 1

Dear Professor X

Dr Y has applied for the post of Lecturer in Discursive Theory in the Department of Miscellaneous Studies at this university and has given your name as a referee.

The Selection Panel for the post wishes to assess how closely Dr Y's qualifications, skills, expertise and experience match the selection criteria as set out in the further particulars, a copy of which is enclosed. The panel would be greatly assisted if, from your knowledge of Dr Y, you were able to give examples of the ways in which s/he will be able to satisfy the requirements of the job description and person specification.

As interviews for the post are to be held on <insert date>, an early reply would be much appreciated. Please feel free to fax an advance copy of your report, using the number given at the top of this letter. As it is not the university's usual practice to acknowledge receipt of references, may I take this opportunity to thank you in advance for your assistance.

Yours etc.

Example 2

Dear Ms A

Mr B has applied for the post of Catering Assistant in our Hospitality Division and has given permission for us to approach you for an employment reference. I should be most grateful if you would complete the enclosed reference questionnaire and return it to me as soon as possible.

As it is not the university's usual practice to acknowledge receipt of references, may I take this opportunity to thank you in advance for your assistance.

Yours etc.

Reference Questionnaire

Name of applicant: Mr B

Date of Birth: 1.1.79.

Dates of employment with your organization: From   To

Capacity in which employed:

Outline of main duties:

Reason for leaving:

Number of days sickness in last 12 months:

Disciplinary record at time of leaving (please give details of any warnings, or ongoing disciplinary action, current at the end of the applicant's employment with you):

Signed: Date:

Name (please print):

Position:

On behalf of:

Interviewing

Setting up the interview

Many universities and colleges will have rules that specify the composition of interview panels for at least some posts. For posts not covered by such local rules, it is good practice to ensure that panels comprise of at least two people. It is also good practice to avoid single-sex or all-white panels, where possible, but members should be chosen for the applicability of their skills and experience, not in a token capacity. A chairperson should be agreed who will facilitate the interview (for more details about the chairperson's role see page 35).

The venue for the interview should be chosen with care to ensure that it is free from distractions and interruptions. If possible, choose a room that is readily accessible for candidates with a physical disability that affects mobility. Prepare the room in advance, giving thought to the physical layout so that candidates do not feel ill at ease (for example, ensure that chairs are all at the same level and that the candidate's chair is not opposite a bright light or window).

Agree a schedule for the programme of interviews, ensuring that each candidate is allocated an adequate and equal period of time. Take account of any additional tests, presentations and visits that have also been arranged and where the candidates are travelling from – you may need to arrange overnight accommodation for candidates travelling some distance. Decide in advance how you will respond if a candidate is unable to attend on the scheduled date. You may decide to proceed with the interviews as arranged and only reconvene the panel if the post is not offered to one of the candidates able to attend on that day. Alternatively, you may decide to stage the interviews and defer a final decision until all the candidates on the original shortlist have been interviewed. If more than one candidate is unable to attend on the scheduled day, ensure that they are treated consistently.

Candidates should be invited to the interview, in writing, with as much notice as possible. The following information should be included:

- the date, time and location of the interview;
- directions to the location, and any relevant car parking or public transport information;
- advance notice of any tests, presentations, visits and so on;
- details of overnight accommodation that has been arranged, if any;
- notice of any documents/information that they should bring with them;
- an invitation for them to advise you of any special arrangements that they will require to be made for the interview;

- a request for permission to approach referees if this has not already been given.

If your organization has a policy of taking up references before interview, then referees for all the shortlisted candidates should be approached, in writing, at this stage. (See page 31 for more information about using references.)

About a week before the interviews are due to take place, send the following information to the interview panel:

- an interview timetable, including details of the venue;
- a copy of the advertisement and further particulars;
- the job description and person specification;
- copies of the applications and supporting documentation;
- copies of any references received.

The interview (the role of the chair, structure, interview skills, note-taking, types of question)

The chairperson will keep proceedings under control and ensure fair play by taking responsibility for:

- ensuring that panel members understand their role in the interviews;
- introducing the panel to the candidates;
- explaining the interview structure to the candidates;
- moving the questioning on;
- as far as possible, keeping the interviews to time, to ensure equity to all candidates;
- dealing with any problems or inappropriate questions;
- closing the interview and explaining the next stage.

Members of the interview panel should meet in advance of the interviews to remind themselves of the requirements of the post and to agree an interview structure. Sufficient time should be allowed at the beginning to put the candidate at ease and for the chairperson to introduce the panel and explain the structure of the interview. Sufficient time should also be left at the end for the candidate to ask questions about the job and the organization (it is helpful to try to anticipate the kinds of question that the candidate might ask and be prepared), and for the chairperson to explain the next stage of the process. The bulk of the interview should be devoted to acquiring information from the candidate and it is important at the planning meeting to clarify the roles of the panel members and to allocate question areas, based on the person specification, according to their expertise. All questions must relate to the requirements of the job and candidates must not be asked about their personal circumstances, family commitments or domestic obligations. It is important that all the candidates are questioned about the same areas covered by the person specification, but this does not mean that all the candidates have to be asked exactly the same question on each topic.

The interview is likely to be more successful if the candidate feels at ease and answers questions freely. For the majority of people, interviewing (or being interviewed) is a relatively infrequent experience and the advice on interviewing skills in Boxes 2.11 and 2.12 may be helpful. Some sample questions, to get you going, are included in the Appendix at the end of the chapter.

Box 2.11 Interviewing tips (1)

- Try to be relaxed and friendly to put the candidate at their ease.
- Concentrate on what the candidate is saying and, as importantly, what they have left unsaid.
- The candidate should do most of the talking – try not to interrupt, unless it is necessary to regain control, in which case, be tactful.
- Give verbal and non-verbal encouragement. It is important that candidates are aware that all the panel members are concentrating on what they have to say, so do maintain eye contact and don't stare out of the window, open your post or do other work during the interview!
- If a candidate is overly verbose, try to regain control by removing non-verbal encouragement (dropping the gaze and so on).
- Watch for non-verbal cues (gestures, changes in posture and so on).
- Cover all aspects of the candidate's application that are relevant to the post and probe any apparent discrepancies.
- Take notes – there will be a lot of information to recall in the decision making process – but try to do it unobtrusively and with the minimum of disruption to eye contact with the candidate. Notes should be factual and reflect information relevant to the post, not subjective impressions or irrelevant detail.

Box 2.12   Interviewing tips (2) – questions

- *Open questions* (that is, ones that begin with 'What', 'Why', 'When', 'Where' and so on) are useful for encouraging candidates to talk and to provide a fuller, more considered reply. Most questions in an interview should be of this type.
- *Closed questions* (that is, ones that require a simple 'Yes' or 'No' answer) should be kept to a minimum and used just to check facts.
- *Probing questions* can be used to explore an issue in more depth. Examples might be 'Could you give me an example?' and 'What happened next?'
- *Leading questions* (that is, ones that give a clear signal as to the 'right' answer) should be avoided as they provide no useful information for the panel.
- *Multiple-headed questions* (for example, 'You've not been in your current post for very long, why do you want to leave at this point, or is it that you want to join our department here?') should also be avoided. They will either confuse the candidate, or will provide an opportunity for them to avoid answering a question they don't like. Either way, the value of a multi-headed question is less than the sum of its parts.
- *Hypothetical questions* (that is, ones that begin 'What would you do if . . .?') help to assess how a candidate would deal with a scenario that they are likely to come across if appointed, but can disadvantage candidates who are unfamiliar with the organization's structure or culture. Also, what candidates say they would do might bear little relation to what they would actually do.
- *Behavioural questions* (for example, 'Think of a project you have managed. What problems did you encounter and how did you overcome them?') seek evidence from the past as an indicator of future performance and are preferable to hypothetical questions.

The decision

The decision making part of the process should be structured so that the candidates are given equal consideration, and it should happen as soon as possible after the interviews. If there were other selection activities (for example, a research seminar for candidates for an academic post or a word processing test for a secretary) there should be an opportunity for feedback on each candidate's performance, to augment the evidence collected during interview. The panel should be asked to compare notes to see how well each candidate matched up to the person specification. Remain objective and avoid 'gut reactions' – you should be prepared and able to justify your decisions if necessary. Be aware of the strength of first impressions and ensure that you give objective consideration to all the evidence, not just how you felt about a candidate in the first few minutes. Candidates should be ranked and gradually eliminated, using evidence from the interview. All being well, the panel will reach a consensus decision, but if unanimity cannot be achieved then a vote should be taken.

Ensure that the decision, and the reasons for it, is recorded in sufficient detail so that it can be justified at a later date, in an employment tribunal if necessary. All the original documentation (including the job description, person specification, advert, applications, details of the shortlisting and the interview notes) should be kept for 12 months after an appointment has been made.

It is possible that, after the interviews, none of the candidates are thought to be suitable. While this can be frustrating, disappointing and inconvenient, don't be tempted to pick the best of a bad bunch. In the longer term, it is better not to appoint than to appoint an unsuitable candidate.

Formulating an offer package and how to break the good (and the bad) news

Formulating an offer package

In HE, with the exception of the most senior posts, there tends to be limited flexibility in terms of formulating a reward package for the successful job applicant. When considering basic salary, refer back to the advertisement – this is one of the things that will have influenced the candidate's decision to apply for the post and they will expect an offer that is at least not inconsistent with the advertised rate. If there is a salary scale associated with the post, ensure that the salary to be offered is appropriate to the qualifications and experience of the candidate and is comparable to that of other people doing similar jobs in the organization. Be aware of equal pay considerations and try not to be overly influenced by the current salary of the candidate – the 'let's just add a little bit to what they're already earning' approach can indirectly discriminate against women by perpetuating existing salary inequalities. When determining the basic salary (and any other benefits, such as cars, health insurance, removal expenses, access to external income and so on) be sure to apply the same criteria in the same way to everyone, irrespective of sex, disability, ethnicity, race, religion and age.

Passing on the good news

You will want to contact the successful candidate as soon as you can after the decision has been made – if they're good enough for you then they're probably good enough for other organizations, too! However, before you make that phone call, it is as well to anticipate those areas that the candidate may wish to have clarified, and to be either armed with the relevant information, or with contact names to cover any gaps. The obvious areas are set out in Box 2.13.

In most organizations, only certain people have the authority to make an offer of employment, so before placing that call you should check whether you are one of them! If you aren't, you should say to the candidate they are to be recommended for appointment and that a formal offer will be issued in the next few days. Explain that you are not authorized to make a formal offer but that you are able to outline, informally, the main terms that will be offered.

Breaking the bad news

You could, of course, opt out of this by saying that only the successful candidate will be contacted by phone. However, unsuccessful candidates can feel that they have been shabbily treated and be left with an

---

Box 2.13   Areas that might come up in the 'good news –
you've got the job!' call

- *Salary* (there might be additions to the basic salary that you will want the candidate to know about – for example, shift allowances, bonuses and so on)
- *Pension* (this will almost certainly be an area where you will want to refer the candidate to a specialist in the organization)
- *Additional benefits* (for example, health insurance, car, interest-free loans for season tickets, help with removal expenses and so on)
- *Starting date* (you should have asked about availability in the interview, so you will have an idea of a realistic start date)
- *Probation* (if it will apply and how long is the probationary period)
- *Working hours/pattern* (particularly important for part-time positions, but increasingly important for full-timers, too)
- *Any special conditions attaching to the offer* (for example, is it subject to satisfactory references or medical clearance)

unfavourable impression of the organization. It also won't stop calls from the eternal optimists who will persuade themselves that the reason they haven't been called is not that they were unsuccessful but because you have been too busy/indisposed/run over by a bus. When calling unsuccessful candidates (and do call, don't use email for this), plan what you are (and are not) going to say in advance. Some candidates will ask for feedback, either on their interview performance or on their application as a whole. Feedback should be constructive and as objective as possible. However, sometimes the decision boils down to one good candidate being a better match for a particular job than another good candidate, and although it does feel a little lame to say so, don't invent feedback. It's a good idea to contact the successful candidate first – if they turn you down immediately you will be able to go to the reserve candidate without embarrassment. If the successful candidate asks for time to consider the offer, or won't give a definite 'yes' until they've received the formal offer, it is as well to be honest with the reserve candidate and explain the situation to them.

Conclusion ■

Once a formal acceptance has been received, you will want to tell the rest of the team, and begin preparations for the new person's arrival. Finding the right person for the job, and persuading them to accept it, is just the beginning. The next steps, which are crucial to the ultimate success of an appointment, are covered in Chapter 3. Further information about recruitment and selection is included in the Appendix to this chapter.

Appendix ■

Job descriptions and person specifications

Example 1: project administrator

Job description
Job title: Project Administrator
Department: Materials Engineering
Grade: Secretarial, Clerical and Ancillary Scales Grade 4
Point: 18–21 depending on qualifications and experience
Salary: up to £15,675 per annum

Job purpose
To provide part-time administrative support to a European Union funded research project in materials engineering.

Outline
The post involves the collating and filing of financial records and technical reports for the project partners based throughout Europe and liaison with both the other partners and the European Commission offices to provide these records, as they are required.

Duties and responsibilities
1 To collate and file technical reports and financial records from the various project partners in both paper and electronic format.
2 To act as a point of contact between the project coordinator, project partners and the European Commission offices regarding the project.
3 To become familiar with the European Union regulations relating to the research project and the records required relating to the project.
4 To process and deal with mail and other communications received relating to the project.
5 To inform the various partners as and when reports fall due and record the receipt of satisfactory reports from the project partners in order to release payments from the university.
6 To attend and minute occasional project steering committee meetings both in the UK and abroad (no more than twice annually).
7 To assist the preparation (word processing and presentation) of technical project reports.
8 To undertake general clerical duties such as photocopying, faxing etc. related to the operation of the project.

Supervision
1 Supervisor: Dr A. N. Other (project coordinator).
2 Level of supervision received:
   – will meet with project coordinator on a weekly basis to discuss planned objectives;
   – will be expected to be capable of working under own initiative and to plan own work to meet these objectives.

Special conditions
1 The contract is part-time at 1/10 of a full-time post (averaging 16 hours per month). However, the nature of this contract entails some flexibility in working patterns to meet the demands of the project. Occasional overseas travel may also be required.

2 The person appointed will be required to sign a non-disclosure agreement with regard to confidential information supplied during the course of the project.

Person specification

Job title: Project Administrator
Department: Materials Engineering

	Essential	Desirable
Experience	Word processing	Note and minute taking Experience of Powerpoint and Excel software
Skills and abilities	*Ability to:*	
	Liaise with UK and overseas research partners by telephone and email to arrange for delivery of financial and technical reports	Familiarity with technical terminology relevant to electrical and/or materials engineering
	Organize project reports and records in appropriate paper and electronic file system	Flexibility to attend occasional overseas research meetings including overnight stays
	Collate and maintain financial records for project in collaboration with university accountant	
	Word-process technical reports	
Education/ qualifications	GCSE-level qualifications in maths and English (grade C or above)	Formal IT qualification such as CLAIT, ECDL

Example 2: lecturer

Department of Computer Science – lecturer

Job purpose

All lecturers are expected to teach on undergraduate and postgraduate modules in the general area of computer science as well as contribute to more specialized computing modules. The successful candidate will also be expected to achieve high quality research in their chosen area of computer science.

Duties and responsibilities
To be employed as a lecturer in the Department of Computer Science. Overall duties and responsibilities will include:

1 Undertaking research in a defined field of computer science, contributing to the department's research profile through published peer reviewed output in journals of international standing.
2 Securing external research funding.
3 Supervising postgraduate students at masters and doctoral levels.
4 Attending appropriate academic and professional conferences, so as to develop an international profile and to contribute to the external visibility of the Department of Computer Science.
5 Lecturing in an area of computer science assigned by the head of department.
6 Provision of tutorial support to computer science students on a variety of teaching programmes within the department.
7 Undertaking necessary academic duties, i.e. supervising project writing, setting examination questions, marking, etc., associated with teaching within a quality department.
8 Visiting students during the placement year of sandwich degree course.
9 Participating in relevant professional activities.
10 Undertaking administrative duties commensurate with experience and situation (e.g. probationary status) within the Department of Computer Science. Such duties may be delegated by the head of department.
11 To take part in and, on occasion, act as chair of one or more of the departmental committees, these responsibilities being equitably distributed across the academic staff.
12 To engage in professional and personal development (e.g. through attendance at relevant training courses offered by the university's Staff Development Unit) which are consistent with the needs and aspirations of the lecturer and the department.
13 To undertake such other duties as may be reasonably requested and that are commensurate with the nature and grade of the post.

Person specification (E = essential, D = desirable)

Education and qualifications

Relevant degree – preferably in computer science	E
Higher degree	D

Research experience

Evidence of research output	E

Key skills

Teaching and presentation	E
Communication	E
Competency in a modern computer language	E

Key aptitudes and personal qualities

Commitment to research and teaching	E
Approachable	E
Enthusiasm	E
Willingness to work as team member and integrate their research interests in line with existing Department of Computer Science activities	E
Self-motivated	E

Example 3: Research Assistant

Job description
Job title: Research Assistant
Department: Materials Engineering
Grade: Research Assistant 1A
Point: 4–7 depending on qualifications and experience
Salary: up to £20,267 per annum

1 Job purpose
To work on a European Union funded project developing new high performance composite magnetic materials incorporating a ceramic and/or ormocer type phase.

2 Project description
The post, which is in collaboration with a number of European and international materials producers, component and electrical goods manufacturers, will involve the use of chemical and powder processing routes, including isostatic pressing and related techniques to derive complex composite structures, together with mechanical, electrical and magnetic property testing of the resultant components.

3 Duties and responsibilities
3.1 To undertake materials and process development for high performance magnetic composite materials and components.
3.2 To work with departmental technical staff and perform appropriate characterizations by optical and electron microscopy, X-ray diffraction, thermal analysis, viscometry, FTIR, together with mechanical and electrical testing as appropriate.

3.3 To undertake the manufacture of laboratory prototype devices.

3.4 To provide detailed records and reports of experiments and results.

3.5 To provide (in collaboration with the academic supervisor) an quarterly progress report for presentation to the project steering committee.

3.6 To assist the academic supervisor in the preparation of agreed publications arising from the work.

3.7 To comply with appropriate health and safety requirements.

3.8 To be responsible for maintaining the laboratory environment and apparatus in a clean and serviceable condition.

4 Supervision

4.1 Supervisor: Dr A. N. Other.

4.2 Level of supervision received:
 – will have weekly progress meetings with academic supervisor at which objectives are reviewed and defined as appropriate;
 – will be expected to be capable of working under own initiative and to plan own work to meet these objectives.

5 Special conditions

5.1 This is a 24-month contract in the first instance. Further extensions may be available, depending on a continuation of funding.

5.2 The person appointed will be required to sign a non disclosure agreement with regard to commercially confidential information supplied during the course of the project.

Person specification

Job title: Research Assistant
Department: Materials Engineering

	Essential	Desirable
Experience	Experience in at least one of the following research areas covered by the project: (i) chemical processing of ceramics and/or hybrids; (ii) magnetic materials; (iii) powder processing routes from metal or ceramic components	Experience in more than one of the research areas covered by the project Experience of electrical measurements

Skills and abilities	Work unsupervised in laboratory on a day-to-day basis	Skilled in use of standard materials characterization techniques
	To maintain confidentiality	Some language skills in French, German or Polish
	To work in a safe and efficient manner	
	To be prepared to undertake routine cleaning of laboratory apparatus and equipment	
	Communicate adequately in written and spoken English	
Education/ qualifications	Degree level qualifications in materials science, chemistry, physics or other closely related subject	PhD in relevant subject

Sample adverts

Staff Development Centre

Senior Clerk
Salary Grade 2 – £10,558 to £12,556 p.a.
Ref: S5069/WEB

A skilled and resourceful person is required to join our busy adminis-trative and secretarial team, reporting to the Chief Clerk. You will be involved in all aspects of the Centre's work, course administration, and providing support to the professional staff.

Essential requirements are good word processing and database skills, attention to detail, the ability to work to tight deadlines, and good inter-personal skills for customer/delegate liaison. You will be involved in the fullest range of office duties.

Informal enquiries are welcome and should be made to the Staff Development Centre office [include email and telephone numbers here].

Downloadable application forms and further particulars are available by following the links above, or in hardcopy from the Personnel Office [insert email, telephone and fax numbers here].

Please note that CVs will only be accepted in support of a fully com-pleted application form.

Closing date: [insert closing date here]

Library

Part-time Library Assistant (17.5 hpw, Monday–Friday or Wednesday–Friday)
Salary Grade 2 – £10,558 to £12,556 *pro rata* p.a.
Ref: SL5010/WEB

You will work as part of a small team to ensure that the library's book stock is maintained in good condition. Duties will include carrying out minor book repairs, covering paperbacks with plastic covers and preparing books for dispatch to external binders. You will have good manual dexterity, the ability to work neatly and quickly with a range of craft tools, and good communication and team-working skills. Minimum qualifications are four GCSEs or equivalent.

Informal enquiries are welcome and should be made to Appointments (Support Staff), Personnel Office [insert email and telephone numbers here].

Downloadable application forms and further particulars are available by following the links above, or in hardcopy from the Personnel Office [insert email, telephone and fax numbers here].

Please note that CVs will only be accepted in support of a fully completed application form.

Closing date: [insert closing date here]

Sample interview questions

'Push' and 'pull' factors
a What is it about this job that attracts you most?
b What elements of your current job do you enjoy most/least?
c Why do you want to move on from your current position?

Experience
a Briefly describe your career so far.
b What aspect of your career so far have you been most proud of?
c Describe how you feel your professional experience so far would help you to do this job.

Skills and abilities

a Describe the most significant written document/report/present-ation that you have had to complete.

b Tell us about a time when you have had to use your verbal com-munication skills to get a point across that was important to you.

c Give us an example of how you had to use your fact-finding skills to solve a problem, then tell us how you analysed the situation to come to a decision.

d Describe the most creative work-related project with which you've been involved.

e Give us an example of a time when you feel you were able to moti-vate your team.

f Have you had to deal with a situation when one of your team wasn't pulling their weight? Tell us how you dealt with the situation.

g Describe a work situation when you have been able to positively influence people in a desired direction.

Other

a Give an example of a time when you had to go above and beyond the call of duty to get a job done.

b Give an example of an important goal that you have set in the past and tell us how you achieved it.

c Have you had to do a job that was particularly uninteresting? Tell us how you dealt with that situation.

d What is your greatest strength/weakness?

e What do you think are the three most important attributes that the person appointed to this job must have? Why?

f What do you think are the attributes of a successful team?

Groups not subject to immigration controls or who are otherwise permitted to work in the UK

- British citizens.
- Commonwealth citizens with the right of abode.
- Nationals of European Economic Area countries (* denotes member of European Union): Austria*, Belgium*, Denmark*, Finland*, France*, Germany*, Greece*, Iceland, Ireland*, Italy*, Liechten-stein, Luxembourg*, Netherlands*, Norway, Portugal*, Spain*, Sweden*.
- Swiss citizens.
- Family members, irrespective of nationality, of non-British Euro-pean Economic Area nationals provided the European Economic

Area national is lawfully residing in the UK and, if the family member is a spouse, the marriage has not ended.
- Asylum seekers who have been given written permission to work.
- Certain people who are appealing against a refusal of an application for further permission to stay. They will have letters from the Home Office confirming that they can be legally employed.
- Student nurses admitted under the terms of the immigration rules who may enter into contracts of employment without any additional permission being required.
- International students registered to undertake study in the UK for six months or more may take vacation employment and part-time employment during terms (up to 20 hours per week) without requiring a work permit (however, there are conditions and advice should be sought from your personnel/HR department).
- No restrictions on the employment of nationals of the following countries from 1 May 2004: Cyprus, Czech Republic, Estonia, Hungary, Latvia, Lithuania, Malta, Poland, Slovakia and Slovenia.

3

MANAGING THE EARLY DAYS

Introduction

Congratulations! You have successfully navigated the recruitment and selection process. An offer has been made and accepted. You're confident that you've found the right person for the job. A start date has been agreed, so you can now tick that one off the list as a job well done and get on with some work. Right? Wrong – all too often a good appointment fails to fulfil its potential if the new starter is just left to sink or swim. By seeing the management of the early phase of a new employee's time with the organization as an extension of the recruitment and selection process, the necessary planning will be completed when the reason for the post, and the skills and experience of the successful applicant, are still fresh in everybody's minds. This will ensure that, when the new employee arrives, they will feel encouraged to see themselves as part of the team right from the beginning.

This chapter looks at the processes you will need to think about when planning for the arrival of a new member of staff:

- induction;
- probation;
- training.

Induction

It's easy to forget how nerve-racking starting a new job can be. Even when somebody knows that their new job is well within their competence they can feel very insecure when surrounded by people who are familiar with the surroundings and with each other. New staff who are left to their own devices will tend not to ask questions (because they don't know what to ask of whom) so it can take weeks for them to discover the most mundane things. Without effective induction, the new member of staff will never properly get to grips with the organization or their role in it. The likely consequences of this include poor morale, poor integration into the team and failure of the new member of staff to achieve their potential in terms of productivity and creativity. The worst case scenario is that the member of staff will leave within a few weeks or months of starting.[1] Effective induction will help the new member of staff to settle in more quickly, enabling them to concentrate on their job rather than on finding their way around.

Your organization may have a general induction programme for all staff, to introduce them to its culture, values and history. For example, staff development at Loughborough University provides a web-based interactive induction programme and also offers a half-day session three times a year at which new staff can meet some key people and (more importantly) each other. The Staff Welfare Division of the University of Leicester issues a comprehensive induction pack to all new staff which includes copies of university policy documents (for example, on equal opportunities in general and race, harassment and disability in particular, and on data protection) and information on a wide range of topics, including the university's staff development programme, child care provision in the locality and car parking. While a general introduction to the organization is going to be useful and new staff should be encouraged to join in, of much greater importance is a local induction programme, appropriate to the complexity of the job and the background of the new staff member. The following suggestions may help.

Before the new member of staff is due to start

Before the new member of staff is due to start, a more experienced colleague in the same staff group should be assigned as a mentor. The mentor's role is to take the new member of staff under their wing in the first few days and to be a point of contact for answering queries and giving advice during the first few months. This role should not be confused with that of the probationary supervisor, which is covered in detail later in this chapter. Advice for mentors' advance preparation is included in Box 3.1.

Arrangements should be made in relation to the new member of

Box 3.1 Mentors' advance preparation

Find out a little about the new member of staff and the job they are coming into from the head of department or recruiting manager (for example, the job or training they are coming from, any previous experience of HE or of the type of work they have been recruited to undertake, the job description for the post they are taking up, who they will be working for, where they will be working in the department, and so on).

Put yourself in the shoes of somebody new to the department and think about the kind of information they are likely to need and questions they might ask. Take steps to fill in any gaps in your knowledge before the new member of staff arrives.

There is a legal obligation to inform *all* new members of staff of certain health and safety information (for example, the fire drill). It should be agreed beforehand whether the mentor is responsible for passing on this information or whether it is for the departmental safety officer to do so.

---

staff's access to the campus, building, department and so on. This may include ordering keys, swipe cards, assigning passwords and arranging for the allocation of a car parking permit.

Arrangements should also be made for the new member of staff's physical environment. For example, office space may need to be allocated and office furniture and equipment ordered, appropriate stationery should be obtained for desk-based jobs, appropriate protective clothing and equipment obtained for laboratory-based, cleaning or craft jobs and computer accounts should be set up if the new member of staff will have access to a computer terminal.

The head of the department, with the line manager, mentor and probationary supervisor of the new member of staff, should prepare an induction programme covering the first month in post. This should cover:

- familiarization with the organization in general (physically and organizationally);
- familiarization with the department (physically and organizationally);
- familiarization with the post and the establishment of initial work-related targets;
- an initial meeting with the probationary supervisor (if the member of staff is on probation);

- the identification of training needs and the development of a training plan.

Take care not to overload the new member of staff with too much information too early in the programme and build in time for them to assimilate the information they have been given. Involving a range of people in the induction programme will be more interesting for the new member of staff, and provide opportunities for them to learn more about the department and organization as a whole, enabling them to see more easily how their role 'fits' into the bigger picture.

An example of an induction programme (based on the notes at Loughborough University) is included in the Appendix to this chapter.

The new member of staff should be advised of where and when to report on their first day, and arrangements made to ensure that there is someone available to welcome them.

Day one

The head of department (or line manager if more appropriate) should welcome the new member of staff and provide them with a copy of the induction programme, giving a brief overview of what it is intended to achieve and how. This would also be a good opportunity to check whether the new member of staff has any outstanding contractual queries.

The new arrival should be introduced to their mentor and they should be acquainted with the domestic aspects of the department (security arrangements, meal breaks, tea/coffee arrangements, toilets, lockers etc.). There should be a discussion about acceptable norms of conduct and appearance (including departmental dress codes, policy on private telephone calls and use of the internet, flexibility in working hours and so on).

Either the mentor or the departmental safety officer should pass on important health and safety information to the new recruit. The extent to which health and safety is discussed will vary depending on the staff group and location of work, from covering the fire evacuation procedure to going through the Control of Substances Harmful to Health (COSHH) regulations and the departmental radiation policy. A list of the health and safety information that should be passed on to a new member of staff is given in Box 3.2.

The new arrival should be introduced to other members of the department, in particular those who they are likely to come into contact with during the course of their work. They will almost certainly

---

> **Box 3.2**   Health and safety – information for new staff
>
> - Fire drill/alarm testing
> - Name(s) and location(s) of trained first aiders
> - University health and safety policies/arrangements including smoking policy
> - Departmental health and safety policies/arrangements
> - Safe use of display screen equipment and risk assessment of workstations
> - Accident reporting procedures
> - Health and safety in laboratories and workshops (if appropriate)
> - Protective clothing (if appropriate)
> - Out of hours working policy
> - Lone working arrangements

not remember very many names, but at least others in the department will recognize them as a new colleague and be able to come to their rescue if need be.

The new member of staff should be given some time to settle into their office/work space during the day to draw breath and assimilate the information they have been given.

The first week

During the first week, opportunities should be available for the new member of staff to meet the rest of the people within and outside the department with whom they will have most contact during the course of their work. Any remaining essential administrative details should be completed and the process of identifying immediate training needs should get underway (see page 68). The first meeting with the probationary supervisor or adviser should take place, although this initial meeting might be a relatively informal 'icebreaker', with a more formal meeting scheduled for later in the month. At the end of the week, the head of department (or line manager) should meet with the new member of staff again to discuss how they have found their first week and whether they have any concerns they wish to raise.

The second, third and fourth weeks

The subsequent weeks of the initial induction period should include:

- a structured introduction to all the main aspects of the job;
- any necessary training needed to ensure that the new member of staff can become effective in the job as quickly as possible (for example, training in any local computer systems or applications with which the new member of staff is unfamiliar; training in the specific laboratory techniques; training in the safe usage of cleaning equipment, and so on);
- further introductions with people outside the department whom it is useful for the new member of staff to know;
- further opportunities for self-directed research into the organization's history, culture and values;
- a formal meeting with the probationary supervisor or adviser (see the section on probation, below).

By the end of their first month in post, the new member of staff should have a clear understanding of:

- the organization's mission, culture and structure;
- their job, and how their role 'fits' into the overall organization;
- who to ask, or where to find information, when they meet new situations or encounter difficulties in their work.

All being well, the new member of staff will be feeling happy, secure and enthusiastic about the organization and their new job.

One way of ensuring that none of the information that should be conveyed to a new starter is overlooked is to use an induction checklist. The induction checklist used by Sheffield Hallam University is included in the Appendix to this chapter as an example of this approach.

Probation ■

Virtually all new staff appointed in a university or college will serve a probationary period. It is not unusual for the duration of the probationary period to vary and it will be specified in the relevant conditions of service. In the pre-1992 universities, academic and some related staff serve a three-year probationary period, while the period for other staff is much shorter, typically six months or a year. In some post-1992 universities and colleges of HE, even academic staff are often only subject to a year's probation.

Managed effectively, the probationary period serves a twofold purpose. It allows the probationer to find their feet in a new job within the context of a supportive framework while allowing the university, as the employer, to be assured that the new member of staff is 'up to the job'. In the majority of cases, the probationary period is completed entirely satisfactorily and the appointment is confirmed. However, in a very small number of cases problems arise which, if not capable of resolution, may lead to an extension of the probationary period or even dismissal.

Target setting, monitoring and evaluation

The employer's responsibility to a probationer, as far as the employment tribunals are concerned, was established many years ago. In the 1977 case of *The Post Office* v. *Mughal*,[2] the Employment Appeals Tribunal (EAT) decided that the employer had to set a standard for employees and give training and feedback. If the employee failed to meet the employer's standard, then they could be lawfully dismissed. The importance of giving training and feedback, as well as setting standards, was emphasized in the case of *Patey* v. *Taylor and Wishart*.[3] Mr Patey, the probationer, was not told about the nature of his duties, or that some of his clients could be difficult. When he was dismissed and claimed unfair dismissal, the EAT found that if an employer had failed to give the employee necessary information relating to their job, feedback on their performance or necessary training, then the dismissal would be unfair.

To be fair, and just as importantly, effective, performance targets should be **SMART**, that is:

- *Specific:* it's no good saying to someone that they must be performing satisfactorily by the end of the week/the month/the year without also telling them what 'satisfactory performance' means.
- *Measurable:* if progress towards a particular target cannot be measured, then how will you judge if the probationer is performing satisfactorily? There should be objective measures of attainment for all targets to minimize subjectivity in the assessment of performance.
- *Attainable:* probationers must not be set up to fail. Setting targets that cannot be achieved is not only grossly unfair, but also bad management. People who feel that they're progressing and making a contribution to the organization will be motivated to take on more responsibility. The converse also applies.
- *Relevant:* targets that are related to the probationer's work will be meaningful and help them to learn more about the job. Arbitrary goals lack credibility and will tend to create the impression that the department doesn't take the probation process seriously – so why should the probationer?

Box 3.3   Some examples of SMART targets for new probationers

- *Academic:* (i) the submission of a fast-stream research grant application to one of the research councils within the first year of employment; (ii) the publication of at least one journal paper, or equivalent, in the first year of employment; (iii) the successful design and delivery of a new third-year option for the second semester of employment; (iv) satisfactory completion of Module 1 of the PG Certificate in Academic Practice (or equivalent).
- *Administrative:* (i) effectively carry out specified secretariat responsibilities without supervision by the end of the academic year (measured by the timeliness and accuracy of the production of agenda, minutes and so on); (ii) complete design and construction of a probation monitoring database by the beginning of the next academic year; (iii) complete appraiser training programme within first three months of employment; (iv) attend the Introductory Course for University Administrators during the first year of employment.
- *Manual:* (i) designated areas cleaned in accordance with minimum agreed service levels by the end of the first month of employment; (ii) competent in the use of specialized cleaning/catering equipment within the first two weeks of employment; (iii) successfully complete relevant health and safety training within first month of appointment; (iv) attend the university's induction event for new staff.
- *Research:* (i) complete literature review within first month of employment; (ii) design and conduct Phase 1 experiments; (iii) draft first quarterly progress report by the end of first three months of employment; (iv) attend workshops on 'Publications Strategies for Research Staff' and 'Managing Your Research Project' during first year of employment.
- *Secretarial:* (i) carry out all primary tasks of post without supervision by end of three months of employment; (ii) competent in the use of all relevant computer applications within the first month of employment; (iii) successfully complete in-house training in customer service; (iv) attend the university's induction event for new staff.
- *Technical:* (i) competent in core experimental techniques within first two months of employment; (ii) competent in the use of specialized equipment within the first two months of employment; (iii) successfully complete relevant health and safety training within first month of appointment; (iv) attend the university's induction event for new staff.

- *Time-limited:* the probationary period is of limited duration and assessments on the probationer's performance must be made within that time. Targets should be set so that the evidence of performance is available for the assessments to be made in good time.

Box 3.3 give some examples for SMART targets for different groups of staff.

The probationer's progress towards the agreed targets should be monitored regularly so that, if problems become apparent, corrective measures can be taken in good time (see the sample monitoring scheme on page 66 for more advice on what to do if the probationer is not making good progress). This regular monitoring will involve a series of formal and informal meetings between the probationer and the probationary supervisor over the course of the probationary period, with reports being made to the head of department at specified intervals.

It is important that at the time the final evaluation of the probationer's performance is made, all the relevant information, including the probationer's views on their progress, is taken into account. Remember that, unless the probation scheme or the contract explicitly states that the member of staff remains on probation until confirmed in post, the appointment will be confirmed by default unless action is taken to either extend the probationary period or to dismiss before the expiration of the original period. Most formal probation schemes specify the period of notice that a probationer will be given of extension or termination. In the absence of a formal scheme, you should endeavour to give no less warning than the notice period specified by the contract of employment. A sample monitoring scheme is given on page 66.

The role of the probationary supervisor

While the responsibility for monitoring an academic probationer's progress tends to be shared between the head of department and a supra-departmental group, ensuring that probation for research and support staff is adequately supervised is the responsibility of the head of department/section. However, they may choose to delegate responsibility for detailed monitoring to the probationary supervisor, who will normally be the probationer's line manager. For example:

- *Research:* the grantholder, or a senior researcher responsible for the day-to-day supervision of the probationer.

- *Technical:* usually the superintendent technician of the department.
- *Secretarial:* usually the departmental administrator or the departmental secretary.
- *Manual:* usually first-level management (for example, domestic supervisor, chef, craft supervisor).

The role of the probationary supervisor in monitoring the probation of research and support staff is crucial, as they are likely to be in more frequent contact with the probationer than the head of department, who will rely on their advice when making the final evaluation of the probationer's performance. The probationary supervisor should start preparing for their role before the probationer's first day, by:

- acquainting themselves with the details of the formal probation scheme, if one applies;
- ensuring that they have a copy of the probationer's job description and person specification (and have read them);
- preparing a draft work plan for the probationer, preferably in writing, which covers the first week, month or quarter, depending on the job (this will give the probationer a greater sense of what they're expected to do right from the start and will provide a framework for the later review meetings).

The probationary supervisor should have a meeting with the probationer within the first two or four weeks (depending on the length of the probationary period) that covers:

- the overall goals for the probationary period and the probationer's detailed work plan for the coming week/month/quarter;
- the standard of work expected;
- training needs;
- the date and time of the next formal review meeting.

By the end of the first meeting, the probationer and probationary supervisor should have agreed the targets in the work plan, identified any immediate training needs and agreed how they are to be met and the date and time of the next formal review meeting. Brief, informal notes of the meeting, particularly of any agreed actions, should be kept.

For probationary periods of six months or less, the probationary supervisor should aim to have at least two formal review meetings with the probationer to monitor progress – one about halfway through the probationary period and the other about a month before the end of the period. A formal note of the meeting should be made and copied to the head of department. It should include:

- objective evidence of progress towards the agreed targets;
- any training undertaken;
- any further training needs identified;
- the probationer's view of their progress.

In addition to the formal review meetings, the probationary supervisor should make time to meet regularly with the probationer on an informal basis.

Academic probation

Historically, a university *was* its academic staff – a collective of self-governing scholars. Even in the twenty-first century business enterprise that is the modern HE institution, it is the academic staff that have the biggest impact on institutional success or failure. Thus, a 1974 national agreement[4] stated, 'the decisions made on its probationary lecturers are amongst the most vital staffing decisions that a university can make'. Academic staff probation is closely monitored in many universities and colleges, so if you are involved with the management of new academic staff in any way you should make sure you are familiar with the mechanism in your own institution. However, the major differences between academic probation in pre- and post-1992 universities are considered below.

Academic probation in pre-1992 universities

The length of the probationary period for academic and some academic related staff in pre-1992 universities often comes as a surprise to new recruits, particularly those who have already had a successful career outside HE. It seems extraordinary to some people that an organization needs three years to assess whether somebody is competent to do the job to which they have been appointed. It might be useful, therefore, to reflect on the origins of this relatively lengthy probationary period. The 1971 Academic and Related Salaries Settlement included the following agreement in relation to lecturers: 'Probationary period to be three years with possible extension to four years in doubtful cases. Training procedures to be improved with thorough review prior to confirmation on the basis of revised and improved procedures and criteria.' Three years later, the working party formed to take the matter forward produced the *National Agreement*

Concerning the Procedure and Criteria to be Used in Connection with the Probation Period for Non-Clinical Academic Staff. The working party concluded that: 'The primary consideration for the employing university in deciding whether or not to retain a person at the conclusion of his [*sic*] probation must be the long-term interests of the university itself, of the other members of its staff, and of its students.' (The use of the masculine form throughout was intended by the working party to include both male and female probationers).

The working party therefore concluded that, for a person to be offered confirmation of appointment following completion of a probationary period, the employing university must be satisfied that:

a) he [*sic*] has satisfactorily engaged in the teaching of prescribed courses and the supervisory and tutorial work assigned to him;
b) he has satisfactorily engaged in research towards the advancement of his subject;
c) he has conscientiously carried out such examining duties and satisfactorily performed such administrative duties as have been required of him; and
d) he shows promise by his work and enterprise of continuing to develop as a university teacher and a scholar.

While confirmation of appointment after two (or, vary rarely) one year of probation is possible, in practice it usually takes three years for the probationer to build a research profile that is sufficiently strong to satisfy a university with a strong research mission of 'b' above.

The 1974 agreement stipulates that where probation has been satisfactorily completed in one university, it is unreasonable for a second probationary period to be imposed by another institution. However, periods of probation successfully completed at post-1992 universities, which are not covered by the 1974 agreement, will not necessarily give remission from probation in a pre-1992 university.

Academic probation in colleges and post-1992 universities

A national collective agreement concluded in 1990/1 between the employers and unions in what was then the polytechnics and colleges sector provided for a 12-month probationary period for academic staff where the lecturer is either a new entrant to teaching in HE or has significantly different job responsibilities. Variations to the terms of the nationally agreed contract of employment have arisen from local agreements (for example, the probationary period of academic staff at Middlesex University is only eight months), and confirmation of local practice should be sought from the personnel section of your institution.

Although the national agreement includes the expectation that all academic staff will engage in 'research and scholarly activity', the predominant purpose of the probationary period is to ascertain that the new lecturer is a competent teacher. To this end, institutions require reports on formal observations of the probationer's teaching practice as part of the assessment process. For example, Middlesex University requires the dean of the relevant school to submit a report on a probationer's suitability that includes two teaching observations which provide a detailed analysis of the teaching observed.

Academic probation – links to professional standards in teaching

In 2003, the Labour government signalled its intention to encourage greater professionalism in HE teaching in England through the introduction of national professional standards and the accreditation of training for new lecturers in teaching skills, in the expectation that, by 2006, all new lecturers would obtain a teaching qualification that met the new standards.[5] However, while the concept of national professional standards for the sector was new, externally accredited training for HE teachers was not. By 2002, over 100 universities and colleges already offered training programmes in HE teaching which had been accredited by the Institute of Learning and Teaching in Higher Education (ILTHE). Successful completion of these programmes, which qualified the member of staff for membership of the ILTHE, was in many cases a requirement for the confirmation of appointment.

The course requirements of these programmes, in terms of contact hours and assessed work, are not insignificant, and those enrolled are also required to undertake a minimum amount of teaching and/or to be involved in certain types of assessment. These factors should be taken into account when determining the probationer's overall workload.

Academic probation – the role of the probationary adviser (mentor)

In academic probation, where judgements about the progress of probationary staff are taken within a formal structure, the role of the probationary adviser (also known as the mentor in some institutions) is to give guidance and support, and to encourage the probationer throughout the period of probation to plan, set and achieve their own objectives/targets. Some suggestions for those advising or mentoring academic probationers are given in Box 3.4.

Box 3.4   Academic probation – what should a probationary adviser do?

- *Give constructive advice/criticism*. You are likely to be one of the first people that a probationer will turn to for advice. It is important that the advice you give is thoughtful and constructive. If you feel that you are not competent to advise on a particular matter, suggest someone who the probationer might approach instead.
- *Meet on a formal basis regularly and give feedback*. You and your probationer should arrange to meet formally several times during the year. At these meetings you should consider progress made against the agreed targets for research, teaching, professional development and administration (if appropriate). If targets are not likely to be met, or training courses were not attended, you should discuss why. Be proactive in arranging meetings, agree an agenda and write the minutes as soon as you can after the meeting. Don't forget to always set a date and time for next meeting.
- *Assist with professional development*. There are a variety of ways in which you can do this. For example, (i) arrange to observe the probationer's teaching, at least twice if possible, during the year (or arrange for a senior colleague to do so), and offer constructive feedback; (ii) advise on the preparation of course material, the setting of exam questions and so on; (iii) advise on the supervision of research students; (iv) arrange for your probationer to observe your teaching and/or that of a senior colleague.
- *Negotiate mentoring time*. Your involvement should go beyond the formal meetings indicated above. You should set aside time, for example, to assist the probationer in the preparation of grant applications, or to discuss the relative merits of different conferences, or to offer information and advice on university procedures (for example, for gathering and analysing student feedback).
- *Give guidance on target journals and lead-in times*. Research outputs, of appropriate quality and quantity, are crucial in demonstrating that the probationer is making good progress. If you are unable to provide this information, perhaps because the probationer's area of research is somewhat removed from your own, find someone who can.

Probation for administrative staff

In pre-1992 universities, staff on academic-related scales (other than research staff) tend to be subject to probationary arrangements analogous to those for academic staff. In colleges and post-1992 universities, the probation arrangements for administrative staff tend to be more closely related to those for secretarial and other support staff. If you are preparing for the arrival of a new member of administrative staff in your department, check what arrangements are in operation in your institution.

Probation for research staff

In 1996, representatives of the UK's universities, colleges of HE and the research councils agreed the *Concordat on Contract Research Staff Career Management*. The signatories to the *Concordat* recognized that only a small minority of contract research staff (CRS) employed in universities and colleges have the opportunity to follow a long-term career in HE, either as researchers or as lecturers, but that very little attempt was made to either manage the career expectations of CRS or to prepare them for life outside the sector. The *Concordat* established a framework for more effective career management and development of research staff employed by universities and colleges on fixed-term contracts funded by research council grants.

The Research Careers Initiative (RCI) was subsequently established to monitor progress in meeting the standards agreed in the *Concordat* and to identify and disseminate examples of good practice in the career management and development of CRS. In 1998, the RCI published *Employing Contract Researchers: A Guide to Best Practice*. The guide states that: '*funders, together with the Universities, should take some responsibility for career management of CRS, both to make them more effective during their contract research, but also to prepare them for work outside the HEIs*'.

The *Guide* advises that a scheme should be put in place for each CRS which reviews performance, provides clear standards and targets, gives support (in the form of mentoring and training) and explains who is responsible for supervision. The guide also suggests that, because of the range of skills required for most research posts, it is not usually possible to make a final judgement on whether performance is satisfactory in less than one year.

The annex to the RCI's *Guide* sets out the responsibilities of CRS, research managers (usually the grantholders), departmental heads and the institution for the career management and development of

---

Box 3.5   Career management of research staff – responsibilities
of research managers[6]

- Discuss career development with CRS at an early stage in their research employment
- Encourage CRS to develop generic and transferable skills in addition to carrying out their research duties (for example, presentation and project management skills)
- Provide opportunities for CRS to obtain experience and training which will help their career development (for example, teaching experience)
- Allow CRS the opportunity to discuss their career aspirations and concerns
- Ensure that CRS receive regular and constructive feedback on performance and advice on career choices
- Involve CRS in decisions which affect their careers
- Ensure that CRS are given the opportunity to develop their knowledge and skills

---

researchers. The responsibilities of research managers are set out in Box 3.5.

All of the research councils make reference to the obligations of institutions and grantholders with regard to ensuring the management and development of research staff in accordance with the standards set by the *Concordat*. The Medical Research Council (MRC) and the Biotechnology and Biological Sciences Research Council (BBSRC), in particular, quote extensively from the *Concordat* and the RCI's *Guide to Best Practice* in their terms and conditions for awards. All the research councils undertake some monitoring of the training and development of CRS funded by grants that they have awarded. As a minimum, final grant reports address CRS development issues. Additionally, some, if not all, research councils send a training and development questionnaire to CRS at the end of the period of employment funded by the grant. The questionnaire addresses the training and career development opportunities provided during the course of the grant and the employment destination of the CRS following completion of the grant.

Probation for support staff

Probation for support staff is often seen by managers as a one-way process – the opportunity to make sure that the new member of staff really is up to the job. Also, the probationary period tends to be relatively short (six months at most). Consequently, the developmental aspect of the probationary period, and the benefits that flow from seeing it as the foundation stone for the member of staff's ongoing development within the organization, are often neglected. However, increasing numbers of institutions, or their constituent parts, are recognizing the value of developing all their staff, not just the 'knowledge workers'. For example, the Residential Organization of Loughborough University achieved Investors in People status in the late 1990s and has a comprehensive development programme for all its staff; the University of Leicester and the University of Newcastle are accredited by the National Examining Board for Supervision and Management (NEBS) to deliver programmes in team leadership skills for staff in supervisory and junior management roles (or those who aspire to take on such roles); Sheffield Hallam University, in partnership with UNISON, offers access to the union's Return to Learn programme, which focuses on developing skills such as writing, investigating, analysing and working with figures. In addition, the Higher Education Staff Development Agency, in partnership with individual institutions, AMICUS and the funding councils, offers regional development programmes for technicians in HE. If you are involved in support staff probation, consult your local personnel/HR and staff development departments with regard to provision in your institution.

Monitoring of probation – a sample scheme

In addition to the frequent informal meetings that probationary supervisors will want to have with their probationers, it is a good idea to have more formal review meetings halfway through and towards the end of the probationary period. The review meetings should be two-way discussions, so remember to encourage feedback from the probationer on how they feel they are performing and are being supported.

At the *interim* review meeting the following matters should be discussed:

- The probationer's progress in achieving the goals set down for the first half of the probationary period.
- Their overall performance, conduct and attitude.
- Additions to the training strategy, if further training needs have been identified.

- If necessary, a restatement of what the department considers to be acceptable levels of performance and/or standards of conduct.

It may be that even at this stage there are doubts that the probationer will be able to successfully complete the probationary period. In this case, the probationer must have their shortcomings clearly explained to them, as well as the consequences of failing to meet the required standards. New goals should be set for the following months and additional departmental support and/or training should be provided. This should be put in writing to the probationer and you should check whether a copy should be sent to your personnel/HR department.

At the *final* review meeting, which should take place no less than one month before the end of the normal probationary period, the following matters should be discussed:

- The probationer's progress in achieving the goals set for the probationary period.
- Their overall performance, conduct and attitude.
- If a recommendation to confirm the probationer's appointment is to be made, arrangements for including them in the appropriate appraisal/developmental review timetable should be agreed.
- If a recommendation to extend the probationary period is to be made, the probationer must have their shortcomings clearly explained to them, as well as the consequences of failing to meet the required standards. New goals should be set for the extended period and additional departmental support and/or training should be provided. This should be put in writing to them and a copy sent to your personnel section. The date(s) of further formal review meeting(s) should also be agreed at this stage.
- If a recommendation to terminate the probationer's employment is to be made, the reasons for that decision must be clearly explained to the probationer and they must be given an opportunity to respond. The reasons for the decision should be put in writing and sent to your personnel/HR department well before the expiry of the normal probationary period. A decision to dismiss would not normally be expected unless problems had been identified at the interim review stage and the appropriate action taken at that time.

Remember – managers should seek advice from personnel/HR professionals at an early stage if an extension to the probationary period or dismissal might be likely and certainly before the final review meeting takes place.

Training

It is rare that someone is appointed who requires absolutely no training in order to do their new job properly, so it is a good idea, even with the best qualified of appointees, to start with the assumption that they will need some training. The initial identification of training needs should take place in the first formal meeting between the probationer and probationary supervisor and then a training strategy should be drawn up to meet the needs identified, with the aim of assisting the probationer to be fully effective in their new role as quickly as possible.

A brief period of work shadowing will be sufficient to meet most training needs, while your staff development unit will almost certainly offer an extensive programme of workshops (including ones on IT topics), but it may be necessary to consider external training options for specialist requirements.

On the job training (OJT) accounts for about half of all training undertaken by employees in the UK.[7] When done well, OJT is good for developing job-specific skills in a relatively inexpensive and flexible way. As much of the training that a new member of staff will undertake will be OJT, it is worth giving the training programme some thought. Involving a range of other staff in providing OJT can have benefits beyond bringing the new member of staff up to speed, by building team spirit, integrating the new person into the wider team more quickly and sharing knowledge throughout the team. Basic points to remember when planning OJT are given in Box 3.6.

Remember that those institutions (or individual departments) involved in Investors in People or ISO9000 projects have an obligation to invest in the professional development of all their staff while the *Concordat on Contract Research Staff Career Management* places

---

Box 3.6 Planning on the job training – some points to remember

- Start with the easiest tasks first, then move on to more complex ones
- Demonstrate what the trainee has to do
- Watch them carry out the task
- Discuss with the trainee what was done, and how it might be done better
- Ask the trainee to repeat the task until it is mastered
- Provide written backup material (in the form of checklists, diagrams etc.) where appropriate

---

Box 3.7   Examples of research staff training

Example 1

Loughborough University offers a half-day workshop, 'Introduction to the Job of Contract Researcher'. Participants are helped to understand the role of CRS in HE, the pitfalls they can encounter and how to avoid them.

Example 2

The University of Newcastle offers NEBS-accredited Introductory Certificate in Management for Contract Research Staff (aimed at CRS on second research contract who wish to take on the role of supervisor or line manager of a research group).

Example 3

The University of Bristol offers a wide range of development courses for CRS including Project Management for Contract Research Staff and a Career Development Workshop.

---

similar obligations on the university or college with regard to researchers supported by external funds (see pages 64–65). Examples of training for research staff are given in Box 3.7.

Conclusion

The first few weeks and months of a new colleague's career in a university or college are crucial. With appropriate advice and training, they will quickly find their feet and begin to make a positive and valuable contribution to their department. Left to flounder, with inadequate support, they will be unable to fulfil their potential and may become so demotivated that they will look for an employer who values them more highly. The costs of replacing someone who leaves after only a short time in post are significant and the cost of advertising is only one element, to which must be added the costs of staff time devoted to selection, training a new recruit and the impact on service delivery and the morale of remaining team members, which is difficult to quantify, but nevertheless real. Time spent on designing well thought out induction and probation programmes is a sound investment. Effective feedback, throughout a person's career, but particularly in the early days with an organization, is essential, and Chapter 4 includes helpful advice on giving feedback and measuring performance.

Appendix ■

Induction and initial training programme – personnel assistant

This is intended as a framework to support you in your first few weeks in post – it is not meant to be a rigid timetable. Your mentor will have an informal meeting with you at the end of each week to review the 'settling-in' process.

When	What	With whom
Day 1	**Welcome** Introductions (office, staff development, payroll, other admin sections) Tour of building Toilets Tea/coffee arrangements Lunch arrangements Keys/security cards Telephone Priority health and safety information (evacuation procedure, smoking policy, name and location of first-aiders)	Colleague A
11.15 a.m.	**Settling into office and reading background information**	
12.30 p.m.	**Lunch**	Mentor and line manager
1.30 p.m.	**Introduction to the job** **Basic role** Role as member of general office team Key elements (correspondence; telephone enquiries; computer records work; clerical work) Relationship with other sections/departments	Colleague B
	Introduction to the PC and software Login passwords	Colleague C

	Word	
	Excel	
	Email	
4.30 p.m.	**Who's who in the university**	Mentor

Day 2

9.00–9.30 a.m.	**Opening/progressing incoming mail**	Colleague A
9.30–10.30 a.m.	**Filing systems**	Colleague B
10.30 a.m.– 12.30 p.m.	**Recruitment administration** Adverts (house style and deadlines) Logging and progressing applications Invite letters Reference requests Hospitality Panel approval Agenda papers	Colleague C
12.30–1.30 p.m.	**Lunch**	
1.30 p.m.	**Work permits** Background to scheme WP1 WP5 Supporting documentation	Colleague C
3.30 p.m.	**Web-based interactive induction package and time to assimilate new information**	Self-directed
Day 3	**Introduction to the computerized personnel system** **Work shadow**	Colleague D Colleague B
12.00–1.00 p.m.	**Lunch**	
1.05–1.55 p.m.	**Publishing on the web: an overview**	Staff development
2.00–4.30 p.m.	**Work shadow**	Colleague C
4.30 p.m.	**Time with line manager**	Line manager

Day 4	Agree individual work objectives Assume role, with ongoing support of team	Line manager
Day 5, 4.30 p.m.	Review of Week 1 and planning for Week 2	Line manager

Other dates for your diary

When	What	With whom
Week 2	**Front page: an introduction** **Review of induction so far** **Bowling (optional social event)**	Staff development Line manager Personnel team
Week 3	**Publishing on the web: beginners** **Personnel team quarterly meeting (half-day in conference centre)**	Staff development Personnel team
Week 4	**Review of first four weeks** **Agree personal development plan**	Line manager Line manager

Example of an induction checklist

Sheffield Hallam University Organization Development Unit

Induction checklist

1. Pre-employment information		
The following information should be provided before the member of staff starts work or assumes the new role	Tick as appropriate	Date completed
Letter of welcome and pre-employment information sent including joining instructions		
Pre-employment visit arranged (if required)		
Personal induction programme planned for week 1		
Work area prepared		

2. **Starting work: Week 1 (all staff)** *The following information should be provided during the first week at work*		
Introduction to manager and/or programme leader		
Introduction to work colleagues		
Introduction to workstation and office		
Line management explained		
Check employment contract and refer queries to manager or HR department		
Salary/wages – date and method of payment, payroll contact no.		
Salary authorization, P45 and pension form sent to payroll		
Personal calls		
Leave entitlement and procedure for taking leave		
Absence reporting procedure and cover arrangements		
Qualifications verified by director of school/ department		
Hours of work and flexitime scheme (if appropriate)		
Code of confidentiality		
Discuss and agree the personal induction programme		

2.1 **Health, safety and security: Day 1 (all staff)** *The following information should be provided during the first week at work*		
No smoking policy explained		
Evacuation procedure explained		

Accident and hazard reporting procedure explained		
Keys issued		
Office security and security of personal belongings		
Arrangements made for collecting ID card (during first week)		
Introduction to departmental safety adviser (DSA) (during first week)		

2.2 Mentoring scheme: Week 1 (academic and research staff)		
Provide information on university mentoring scheme		
Provide name of mentor		

2.3 Additional information for teaching staff: Week 1 *The following information should be provided during the first four weeks at work*		
Tutor's guide		
Assessment regulations		
The 'Associate Lecturer' information pack		

3. Settling in: Weeks 1 to 4 (all staff) *The following information should be provided during the first four weeks at work*		
University, school/department and team vision, objectives and current priorities explained		
Annual planning priorities and targets explained		
Individual work objectives agreed		
Relationships to other sections/departments/schools		

Key events and timetables		
Team briefings and meetings		
School/department newsletters, notice boards		

3.1 Staff development: Weeks 1 to 4 (all staff) *The following information should be provided during the first four weeks at work*		
Initial personal development plan drawn up		
Staff development opportunities explained		
Appraisal scheme explained		

3.2 Information technology facilities: Weeks 1 to 4 (all staff) *The following information should be provided during the first four weeks at work*		
Connection to network		
Email address		
Training on relevant software		
Security and data protection		
Standard templates – letters, memos, etc.		

3.3 Review of induction and planning ahead		
Review of induction after two weeks		
Review of induction after two months		
Individual work objectives agreed		
Personal development plan agreed		

4

MANAGING FOR PERFORMANCE – TODAY AND TOMORROW

Robin Middlehurst and Tom Kennie

Introduction

This chapter considers the all-important but challenging area of managing for performance in HE. The topic is important in HE for the same reasons as in any other sector or organization: because the performance of individuals and groups is directly related to the success of the institution in delivering its mission and objectives. High performing staff will contribute to a high quality experience for students, and will produce valuable research and a range of services to business and the community. Effective performance at all levels also has wider benefits. Internally, it builds morale as individuals and groups demonstrate a clear sense of purpose and direction, and over time a culture is created that attracts new staff. Externally, effective performance builds a reputation that will attract investment and new clients.

Managing for performance in HE is challenging, however, for three main reasons. The first challenge arises from the scale and scope of university and college operations: institutions are typically (though not uniquely) large and complex businesses. They employ staff from all the standard occupational categories and these individuals are on different contracts and conditions of service, are represented by different trade unions and may be part of national or local pay schemes. Their contributions to the institution differ and are often valued differently in terms of formal reward schemes and informal cultural hierarchies. While there are some general expectations about performance across staff categories, the nature of roles and tasks in the institution will also necessitate differences. Closely linked to this issue is the fact that HE has multiple goals, some of which may be in conflict with one another. This means that at individual and group levels, successful performance is likely to be multi-dimensional. As a consequence of these complexities, managing for performance is itself a complex task.

The second challenge involves the impact of a fast-changing world. Given changes in the external context of HE, at regional and national levels as well as internationally, the precise nature of 'performance' is shifting. The kinds of performance that might have been expected five years ago are not the same as those to be expected in five years' time. Managing for performance must therefore be a dynamic process that focuses on current and future requirements.

The third challenge arises from the culture of HE. The nineteenth-century roots of present management thought and practice[1] lie in the world of industry and commerce; these ideas have only formally entered into the discourse and mainstream organization of universities in the last 30 years. The concept and practice of 'management' has not been greeted with universal enthusiasm; indeed, it is often labelled as 'managerialism', a term of distrust rather than approbation.[2] Hierarchical notions of management emanating from old-style industries with emphases on 'command and control' behaviours are contrasted with university traditions of 'collegiality', with their flatter structures and shared governance arrangements. Ideas about performance in these two traditions also differ. From a collegial perspective, effective performance is assumed to arise from intrinsic motivation and ingrained professionalism. In contrast, a managerialist approach is perceived (by some) to depend on extrinsic motivators and the monitoring of work by managers. Notions of 'managing for performance' can therefore give rise to tensions at a conceptual and practical level. These issues will be discussed further in the sections that follow.

Organization of the chapter

The chapter is organized into four sections. The first sets out the context for performance in UK HE and addresses why managing for performance is a topical issue in HE today. The second builds on the first and focuses more closely on the nature of performance and the concepts underpinning performance management frameworks. The third section focuses on practices and techniques for achieving high performance at individual and group levels. The fourth discusses certain issues in 'managing for performance' in HE before reaching overall conclusions.

Context   ▪

The external environment in which HE institutions operate is changing at international, regional and national levels. We shall briefly explore each level in turn and then illustrate some of the potential impacts on what counts as 'performance' and the task of managing for performance.

International perspectives

At international level, HE analysts have noted that some of the forces for change show remarkable similarities across the globe.[3] These authors note four specific trends that seem to be having widespread impact. They are: expanding enrolments in HE; the growth of new competitors, virtual education and consortia of institutions; the global activity of many institutions; and the tendency for policy makers to use market forces as levers for change in HE.

While expanding enrolments are a global phenomenon, numbers vary greatly across countries, as do the strategies adopted by governments to cope with these levels of demand and need. Current strategies include sending students abroad, supporting the development of private and for-profit institutions, facilitating twinning or franchising arrangements and encouraging branch campuses as well as the development of distance learning.

The emergence of new competitors, virtual universities and consortia is a response to the increases in global demand for HE as well as a response to wider economic and technological trends.[4] UK universities have been in the forefront of transnational education, working from a strong tradition of international engagement. The UK is the world's second highest importer of international students, UK universities are involved in international consortia such as Universitas 21 or the Worldwide University Network and they also serve large numbers of students overseas. The Open University, for example, serves 260,000 students in 41 countries, while other institutions have branch campuses, franchises or twinning arrangements; and many are also investing in e-learning.

Governments' use of market forces as a lever for change in UK HE is noticeable in several areas. The first is funding, where the unit of resource for teaching has been steadily reduced for a decade or more. The recent White Paper on HE records that the funding per student fell 36 per cent between 1989 and 1997.[5] The reduction has been accompanied by government encouragement for institutions to seek alternative sources of income and to be more entrepreneurial. In parallel with reductions in public funding, the size of HE has increased (including the 1992 translation of polytechnics to universities). For example, in 1962 only around 6 per cent of those under 21 participated in HE; by 2002, 43 per cent of those aged 18 to 30 went to university.[6] These expansion and resource pressures have been accompanied by a stronger government emphasis on accountability, manifested both through external arrangements for quality review through the Quality Assurance Agency for Higher Education and by the monitoring of institutional strategies through the funding councils.

Since 1997 and the advent of a new governing party, the use of market forces has been accompanied by ministerial pressure to achieve particular institutional performance targets. For example, the prime minister has set a target to increase the UK's share of the international student market from 17 per cent to 25 per cent by 2005. The Department for Education and Skills has set a target (in England and Wales) to increase participation in HE so that by 2010, 50 per cent of those aged 18–30 will have had experience of HE.[7]

The performance implications of these developments are clear at both organizational and individual levels. Institutions must be competitive in a global context and therefore their staff must be innovative, customer responsive and entrepreneurial. At the same time, institutions are expected to achieve national public policy targets and respond to government expectations of accountability. Internal systems of target-setting, monitoring and recording of performance are emerging in response to this 'performance agenda'.

Regional developments

The UK's membership of the European Union affects HE at a number of levels. Institutions are involved in the European Commission's research frameworks, they take part in a range of development projects, are involved in European networks and consortia to create joint programmes, and they support the mobility of staff and students across Europe through programmes such as Leonardo and Socrates. The European Union is already affecting HE policy and practice through legislation on employment practices (for example, race relations, disability rights, health and safety practices, human rights and employment rights for contract researchers). Developments such as the Lisbon Convention and Bologna Process (which involve developing common structures of HE and a common quality culture) are also likely to bring about more significant changes in the medium term in relation to institutions' awards, curricula and quality assurance arrangements.

The European Commission has also focused attention on the development of regions in Europe as an aspect of economic growth and social regeneration. In the UK, the emphasis on regionalism has been accompanied by two significant developments. The first is devolution of authority from the Westminster Parliament to other parliaments or assemblies in the UK (Scotland, Wales and Northern Ireland). The second involves changes in local government arrangements within England, to focus on regional authorities with a range of responsibilities including support for economic development and funding for the delivery of post-secondary training and education outside universities.

HE is seen by governments in the devolved systems as a key player in regional development and, as 'the regional agenda' has taken hold, institutions have been involved both in regional restructuring agendas and in delivering a range of economic and social benefits to the regions.[8] Specific funds have been earmarked for engagement with business and the community (for example, the Higher Education Funding Council for England's (HEFCE) Higher Education Reach-out to Business and the Community fund). The Regional Development Agencies established in 1999 now offer valuable sources of funding for institutional projects. Liaison and representation at regional levels is as important to institutions as engagement at national level.

The performance implications of developments at regional level are similar to those defined by the international context. However, an important additional point is that institutions must give attention and resources to both levels. Where resources are scarce, individuals may be carrying multiple roles. These roles will require a wide range of skills and capabilities and may also result in significant pressures on individuals' use of time. The process of 'managing for performance' and the design of performance management systems will need to be sensitive to these issues.

National developments

As we have discussed above, government policies have clearly played a part in shaping institutional performance targets at international and regional levels. Recognizing that these political agendas – and the wider context – are likely to require institutions to change their practice in a range of ways, the different jurisdictions of the UK are also placing strong emphasis on enhancing leadership, governance and management in HE. The focus on these territories is not restricted to

HE; it is part of a wider economic agenda to improve leadership and management in all sectors of the UK. Between 2000 and 2002, the vehicle for promulgating this agenda was the Council for Excellence in Management and Leadership (CEML) established by the Department of Trade and Industry and the Department for Education and Skills.

The CEML undertook extensive research on management development and business improvement practices in large and small organizations, on management education supplied by business schools, on management and leadership development in the public sector and on management learning in the professions. The rationale for all this attention was the relationship between management and leadership and organizational performance. This relationship, various reports have noted, is key to workforce development,[9] is a driver of best practice and innovation[10] and is pivotal to investment, productivity, delivery of service and quality of performance.[11]

In HE, the representative bodies and the funding councils are also seeking to enhance leadership, governance and management. In addition, the funding bodies have launched initiatives to develop and improve human resource strategies and practices in institutions. These initiatives deserve special mention because performance management is an important part of them. The key priorities that the funding bodies wish to see addressed in institutions' strategies include: recruitment and retention; staff development and training; equal opportunities; reviews of staffing needs; annual performance reviews; and action to tackle poor performance.

It is clear from the discussion of the national picture that the task of 'managing for performance' in HE is central to government and funding body agendas. The wider changes affecting the environment and activities of institutions support the need for performance management frameworks, but also highlight the range of pressures that will affect the process of 'managing for performance'.

Performance and performance management ■

The nature of performance

As discussed above, the nature of performance will differ among categories of staff, across different levels of the organization, in relation to different roles and tasks and will be subject to change over time. Despite these operational differences, it is possible at a more fundamental level to identify the components of 'performance'.

Performance involves two things: achieving something – a

'performance' (outputs, goals or results) – and *the process* of achieving something (the carrying out of an activity). As Brumbrach[12] suggests, performance is therefore about behaviour and results. Within organizations, the term can be applied at several levels: organizational, group, team and individual, and a performance management framework will typically seek to achieve alignment between the different levels.

In an organizational context, the notion of performance (of the whole organization and of individuals and groups within it) is neither static nor neutral. Instead, 'performance' is dynamic, involving movement from point A to point B. Because of this dynamic, performance can also be measured in terms of the distance travelled from point A to point B and judgements can be made about what behaviours were effective, how results were achieved and what effects were produced. For example, performance can be described as high or low, actual or potential, satisfactory or improving, sustained or declining, producing positive or negative outcomes and impact.

Performance is dynamic in another sense (see Figure 4.1). This is because 'achieving something' and 'the process of achieving something' each involve complex interactions between a number of variables.

Inputs + processes ⇒ performance

Figure 4.1 The dynamic of performance

Variables that contribute to organizational performance include inputs (for example, tangible resources such as finance, physical assets and people, and intangible resources such as shared values and culture, reputation and history) and processes (for example, systems, structures and procedures). At an individual level, inputs include skills, attitudes and motivation, and processes include leadership, formal and informal relationships, and work practices. There is also an interaction between organizational and individual levels. The organization creates the conditions that support or inhibit performance at individual and group levels, and performance at individual and group levels together produce performance at the organizational level. And at both levels, as we have seen above, the wider environment will influence performance by causing shifts in expectations of behaviour and results. Managing for performance therefore needs to be understood as a holistic process that involves leading and managing the organization in the context of its own mission and business objectives and its own internal and external environments (see Figure 4.2). As Armstrong[13] writes: 'Performance is achieved by people and

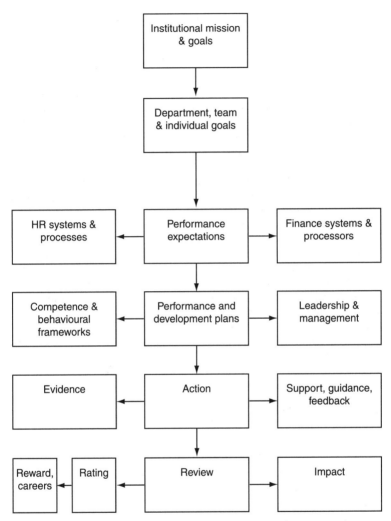

Figure 4.2   A holistic view of managing for performance
(Adapted from Armstrong 2000)

the results they attain will depend upon the quality of leadership they
receive, their motivation, their understanding of what is expected of
them, their knowledge, competence and skill, and the system of work
that affects them.'

Managing for performance and performance management

At this point, we need to distinguish between 'managing for performance' and 'performance management'. The former, we suggest, is a broad concept that involves a relationship between individuals or groups and those who lead them, set in a context of HR systems and practices, and organizational mission and values. A 'performance management system' sits within this broad concept; it includes the specific processes and techniques that are used to establish and assess performance.

Authors place different emphases on the key elements of managing for performance. Armstrong[14] focuses on it as 'a systematic approach to improving and developing the performance and competence of individuals and teams in order to increase overall organisational effectiveness'. The Institute of Personnel Management[15] identifies it as 'a philosophy . . . for achieving a shared vision of the purpose and aims of the organisation, helping each individual employee to understand and recognise their part in contributing to those aims . . .' Despite differences in emphasis, however, there is general agreement that any performance management system cannot be isolated from the prevailing culture, strategies, values and objectives of the organization. Approaches to performance management must also be closely integrated with the wider management systems of the organization;[16] they will depend for success on 'a bundle' of linked HR practices[17] including:

- corporate and departmental planning and control systems;
- finance, resource allocation and budgetary control;
- recruitment and retention;
- job descriptions and job evaluation;
- salary and grading;
- training and development;
- promotion and succession planning;
- discipline and grievance procedures.

Managing for performance as an active process will involve negotiation and agreement between managers (as leaders) and the individuals and teams with whom they work. This shared process is based on the principles of 'contract' and 'joint accountability' rather than command and control[18] and will involve discussion about the goals which managers, teams and individuals wish to achieve and the performance that is required to achieve them, individually and collectively. The major difference between past approaches to managing

people in HE and what is now expected is that the 'performance contract' and the process of producing and achieving it is to be formalized, made explicit and actively managed across the institution, for all
categories of staff. The emphasis is firmly on the creation of a performance management system.

The principles of managing for performance can be summarized as
in Box 4.1.[19] From this summary it is clear that managing for performance is about improvement, development, satisfying organizational
as well as individual goals and building a climate of communication,
involvement, mutual understanding and feedback. There are also
some key ethical issues that should form part of the process:[20]

- *Respect for the individual* (in terms of their rights, needs and
  responsibilities).
- *Mutual respect between parties* (in relation to the different needs and
  preoccupations of those involved in performance management
  processes).
- *Procedural fairness* (the procedures used should operate fairly so as
  to limit any adverse effects on individuals).

Box 4.1   Principles of managing for performance

- It translates corporate goals into individual, team, department
  and divisional goals
- It helps to clarify corporate goals
- It is a continuous and evolutionary process, in which perform-
  ance improves over time
- It relies on consensus and cooperation rather than control or
  coercion
- It creates a shared understanding of what is required to improve
  performance and how this will be achieved
- It encourages self-management of individual performance
- It requires a management style that is open and honest and
  encourages two-way communication between superiors and
  subordinates
- It requires continuous feedback
- Feedback loops enable the experiences and knowledge gained
  on the job by individuals to modify corporate objectives
- It measures and assesses all performance against jointly agreed
  goals
- It should apply to all staff; and it is not primarily concerned with
  linking performance to financial reward

- *Transparency* (the basis and evidence on which decisions are made must be clear and open with opportunities for scrutiny by relevant parties).

Within and outside HE, there are now several organizational frameworks that can assist the task of managing for performance. Two frameworks that are in widespread use are the Business Excellence/ EFQM Model (www.efqm.org) and the Investors in People Standard (www.iipuk.co.uk) These frameworks offer a systematic approach to people management that includes a focus on performance management. The Investors in People Standard is based on four key principles:

- *commitment* to invest in people to achieve business goals;
- *planning* how skills, individuals and teams are to be developed to achieve these goals;
- *action* to develop and use necessary skills in a well defined and continuing programme directly tied to business objectives;
- *evaluating* outcomes of training and development for individuals' progress towards goals, the value achieved and future needs.

These four key principles are a cyclical process and are broken down into 12 indicators against which organizations wishing to be recognized as 'Investors in People' are assessed. The Business Excellence/ EFQM Model was developed by the European Foundation for Quality Management (EFQM). Using a standard conceptual framework (see Figure 4.3), various key aspects of organizational functioning are set out. Each aspect includes a set of indicators that can be measured; in the assessment framework, each area is weighted differently in terms of its relationship to overall organizational effectiveness. The model can be used for self-assessment, for comparative assessment (through benchmarking against other organizations) and for external assessment. It is now the most widely used organizational framework in Europe and has become the basis for the majority of national and regional quality awards.

Performance management systems in a context of change

The picture described above presents a rational and linear perspective of performance management which has clear roots in the philosophy of 'scientific management'.[21] Arguably, this picture does not take sufficient account of new scientific theory,[22] postmodernism as a prevailing cultural dynamic[23] and of the general impact of change on HE

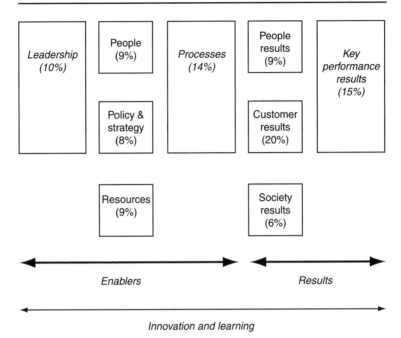

Figure 4.3   The Business Excellence/EFQM Model

practice. Jones[24] argues that the territory of performance management has changed in terms of organizational complexity and individual aspirations and that these changes affect managers and individuals alike. Managers are working in more complex and messy structures such as matrix or networked systems. Teams may be geographically or functionally dispersed, working on projects that operate in different markets under different market conditions. In HE, this will be true of people working on international research projects or international student recruitment as well as those concerned with reaching out to business and the community at regional levels.

At the individual level, the psychological contract[25] between employees and employers is changing. The security of a job for life is no longer a general expectation for individuals (although this expectation remains entrenched at some levels of HE). Autonomy, flexibility, varied and stimulating work, with opportunities to develop skills that will enhance employability are now widespread expectations. Quality of life is also an important driver with implications for the work-life balance in organizations. Some of these expectations have long been part of the experience of academics in HE; as the external environment changes they are now shared expectations across many, if not all, categories of staff. Performance management systems need to be shaped with these expectations in mind.

Outside HE, organizations are reshaping their performance management arrangements in different ways in response to environmental changes. Examples reported by Jones[26] are interesting in that they illustrate changes in management arrangements generally, as well as specific changes in relation to performance management. Her examples include:

- *Syntegra, part of British Telecommunications:* people belong to skill groups that nurture the personal and professional development of members and work in project-focused teams. They set their own objectives and take responsibility for self-managed learning.
- *BBC Worldwide:* individuals are responsible for their own performance and managers assist through coaching and mentoring. Managers carry responsibility for the key training and development needs in their area; they are themselves trained in coaching skills.
- *St Luke's Communications*, an advertising agency: managers are a resource for projects and team members who work directly with clients. Client feedback, press comments and financial achievements are monitored, and each month employees publicly evaluate their work to monitor progress and get feedback from colleagues. In addition, there is a biannual review to help individuals develop their role and aspirations in the business – this takes place with a line manager and a colleague. The job of the colleague is to collect qualitative feedback from others that helps to set the context for the meeting.

Recent research reported by Jones[27] confirms the shifts that are occurring in the territory of performance management. Two important findings are worth noting. The first is the emphasis placed on the *quality* of the dialogue between managers and individuals and between individuals and team members. The second is that the real impact of performance management systems lies as much, if not more, in the way they are *delivered* as in the way they are designed. The need for a commitment to people management and the skills to motivate and support people is critical to successful 'managing for performance' which is in turn a clear source of competitive advantage and an essential tool in attracting and retaining talented people.

Another recent piece of research undertaken in the schools' sector[28] makes a similar case, drawing on case studies of performance management schemes in Toyota, the Derbyshire Building Society and the

Royal Air Force and comparing these with experiences of performance management systems in schools. The findings of this study emphasize that performance management systems need to be an integral part of quality assurance, support and training throughout the organization and must be embedded in working practices and routines. The author also notes that 'Crucially, however, performance management will only flourish where the organisation has a strong value system, a powerful vision and recognition of the crucial importance of leadership at all levels. If the success of these organisations is indicative, the "people-centred" rather than the task oriented organisation appears to offer the most appropriate way forward.' This is an important point for HE since the pressure to deliver 'more with less' in recent years has fostered strong task cultures in many institutions at the expense of people-centred cultures.[29]

Practices and techniques for achieving high performance ▮

In the previous sections we have looked at the environmental context in which managing for performance is taking and will take place and the conditions that help to create an effective performance framework at organizational, group and individual levels. In this section we shift to the 'micro level' of the practices and techniques involved in managing for performance – that is, the 'performance management system'.

The performance management system

Most authors agree that managing for performance at the individual and group or team levels involves a continuing and dynamic conversation between 'managers' and 'staff' (or between professional and professionals). It is not a one-off appraisal. The performance management system can be described as a cycle: two versions are shown in Figure 4.4 to illustrate the difference between a simple management model and a leadership approach.

Within this cycle there are a number of core, 'hard' components as well as a number of important 'soft' components (see Table 4.1 for examples). These components will usually be formalized through written documents, but they will also need to be part of the lived values and practices of the organization. It is important to recognize that the wider concept of 'managing for performance' involves a mix of systematic and disciplined procedures as well as inspiration and commitment to ideas, values and people in practice; one without the

Figure 4.4   Performance management cycles

other will fail to achieve 'high performance'. Critical success factors in the process include:

- *Factor 1:* that expectations of performance are made explicit (in terms of behaviour and results).
- *Factor 2:* that these expectations are formally agreed and supported throughout the organization.
- *Factor 3:* that there is alignment between expectations of performance and wider HR, training and quality assurance systems and practices, as well as alignment with wider leadership behaviours and cultural values.
- *Factor 4:* that leaders and managers at all levels understand and agree their own role in managing for performance and are skilful (and supported) in exercising this role.
- *Factor 5:* that performance criteria are clear, agreed, understood and communicated.
- *Factor 6:* that performance review is evidence based.
- *Factor 7:* that there are consequences that flow from the performance management process. This means that good performance is recognized and supported or rewarded; that poor performance is recognized and dealt with; and that effective individual and group performance is publicly acknowledged as the basis of successful organizational performance (thus achieving wider resource and reputational gains).

Table 4.1 Hard and soft components of performance management cycles

'Hard' components	'Soft' components
Institutional mission and strategic goals	Institutional philosophy and values
Business and departmental goals; team targets; key result areas	Departmental philosophy and values
Aims and objectives of the performance management framework and performance management process	Performance and development negotiations and agreements
Competence framework – linked to selection and training systems and quality assurance	Competence expectations and standards established through leadership and professional practice
Behavioural framework – linked to selection and training systems and quality assurance	Behavioural expectations and standards established through leadership and professional practice
Agreed standards and criteria: statement of performance, classifications of judgement and gradings	Commitment to and engagement with criteria
Planning processes: objectives and targets set, evidence requirements identified (short–medium term)	Negotiation and agreements reached; motivation and commitment harnessed
Monitoring processes	Ongoing leadership and management support for achieving objectives and targets
Short–medium term review processes: evidence-based rating/grading	Feedback, analysis, evaluation, reflection, joint agreement
Recording and reporting	Outcomes emerge; impact of outcomes on performance; support and reinforcement of practice
Future-focused review: training, promotion, careers, succession planning	Evaluation, analysis, motivation, aspirations and projections

Processes and procedures in a performance management system

There are a number of component parts to a performance management system, as follows.

Stage 1: planning and defining expectations

- *Key result areas:* these are the main results or outputs that are expected from the job or task. They need to be discussed and defined between managers and staff (that is, the professionals involved).
- *Performance indicators or measures:* these are the areas of the job or task that can be measured. They may include finance (income earned or added value achieved), outputs (products or services produced), impact (attainment of a standard, changes in behaviour, innovation), reaction (judgement by others), and time (speed of response or turnaround).
- *Objectives:* these are the specific targets to be achieved. They should be linked to business or departmental priorities, be linked to results, be specific and measurable, be challenging but attainable, be time-bounded and updated when necessary.
- *Standards:* these are the criteria or yardstick(s) against which judgements of acceptable performance can be made.
- *Competences:* these are the behaviours, attitudes and skills that are defined by the institution or department as the way a job or task should be performed.
- *Performance and development agreements:* these set out the work to be done, the results to be attained, the performance standards to be achieved and the competence levels required.
- *Action plans, performance and development plans:* these are a joint exploration of what individuals and teams need to do and know to achieve and improve performance and develop their skills, and how managers can provide support and guidance.

Stage 2: action accompanied by active leadership and management

- *Coaching:* this is a structured process whereby managers (or external professionals) provide guidance, support and feedback to assist individuals and teams in building confidence to achieve tasks and perform well, and to develop new skills.
- *Mentoring:* this is a structured process whereby an individual practitioner (usually senior) with particular skills, experiences or strengths is matched with an individual wishing to learn from such experience through structured dialogue and observation.
- *Delegation:* this is a formal process whereby a manager gives a role or task to a member of staff to undertake. It can be used in the context of general management arrangements or as a specific developmental tool.

Stage 3: monitoring performance

- *Feedback:* this involves collecting and discussing the evidence of performance, in terms of behaviour and results, on an ongoing basis. Individuals, teams and managers will collect feedback both formally and informally. Feedback can provide a measure of how closely behaviour and achievement matches objectives and other expectations, of how behaviour has affected others and an overall perspective on how an individual or team is viewed. Feedback should be specific, descriptive, timely and evidence-based.

Stage 4: reviewing performance

- *Appraisal and review processes:* these provide an opportunity for structured feedback, discussion and reflection between individuals and teams and their managers. Evidence of performance will be discussed against performance indicators and standards. A report including judgements (and/or gradings) of performance will usually be produced. The outcomes of formal review processes may be linked to promotion and reward.
- *360-degree review processes:* these involve the structured collection of data (by means of a questionnaire) about performance. Data is collected from three sources: line managers, peers and direct reports. The data, compiled into a composite report, may be used to judge performance or as a developmental tool.

Issues in operating performance management systems ■

There are a number of issues that arise in relation to the operation of performance management systems. These can affect any stage of the process. For example, performance expectations may not be clearly articulated, objectives may not be realistic, gradings of performance may be open to debate and the outcomes of performance reviews may be contentious if linked to promotion or pay. In this section we focus on two particular issues that are important in relation to managing for performance: giving feedback and measuring performance. They are two areas that can have very positive or very negative effects.

Giving feedback

Providing feedback on performance is one of the most crucial roles played by managers and leaders. The task of giving feedback on positive performance is regarded as easy (although in practice it is not always done, or is not done effectively). Giving feedback on poor or less than satisfactory performance is often perceived as difficult and therefore to be avoided. Research by Manzoni and Barsoux shows what can go wrong and how to put things right. In the first study,[30] the authors draw attention to the manager's potential contribution to poor or less than adequate performance; they describe this as the 'set-up-to-fail syndrome'. The syndrome involves a dynamic in which employees perceived to be mediocre or weak performers 'live down' to the low expectations that their managers have of them. The opposite is 'the Pygmalion effect' where good performers live up to high expectations from their managers. In the set-up-to-fail syndrome, a downward cycle is put in motion when the manager notes and assumes that performance is not satisfactory and gives more time and attention to the member of staff, perhaps placing conditions on the work to be produced or critiquing the work more intensely. The heightened supervision is interpreted as a lack of trust and may lead to loss of confidence and motivation on the part of the staff member. This, in turn, is seen as further evidence of poor performance. A further danger is the comparison that is made with higher performing individuals both by the manager and the member of staff. The process can be self-fulfilling and self-reinforcing in both directions: high performers are treated with trust, confidence and ease in relationships while the poor performer suffers from excessive attention and withdrawal of interpersonal connections. As a consequence, the member of staff may themselves withdraw from relationships with the manager or may strive too hard to change the manager's impression of them by overreaching themselves. This leads to further pressure and control on the manager's part and frustration, anger or departure on the part of the staff member.

The solution to the syndrome involves five components, the researchers suggest. The first is to recognize the problem and to set the right context for a discussion of the issues. Both parties must then use the intervention process to come to an agreement on the symptoms of the problem. Third, they need to work towards a common understanding of what might be causing weaker performance in some areas. Fourth, they need to agree on a set of performance objectives that may include managing their own relationship better. Finally, there needs to be an agreement about more open communication – and testing of perceptions and assumptions – in the future. Alongside these practical steps, the authors draw conclusions about how to prevent the set-up-to-fail syndrome. They note that successful managers are actively involved with all employees, although they may behave differently to different individuals. They may reduce their interventions based on evidence of good performance, but where they retain their involvement they do so without disempowering or discouraging individuals. They create an environment in which people feel comfortable discussing performance *and* relationships. These managers also challenge their own attitudes and assumptions about people and their reasoning processes, checking that they are being objective and that they have evidence to support their interventions. Perhaps most importantly, the authors note that successful management involves considerable emotional investment from managers. This level of engagement is key to helping staff reach their full potential.

In the second paper,[31] Manzoni draws attention to other aspects of the feedback process, pointing to the importance of 'open framing' rather than narrow or closed framing of the process. Open framing involves wide-ranging discussion of issues, the seeking of appropriate and relevant evidence and negotiation about understandings and commitments on both sides. Open framing also needs managers and their staff to recognize when particular biases come into play so that alternative explanations can be tested and considered. Manzoni notes that feedback is accepted more willingly when:

- the person giving feedback is reliable and is perceived as having good intentions towards the individual concerned;
- the feedback development process is fair – that is, relevant information is collected, clarifications and explanations are sought and given, the member of staff's opinions are considered and consistent standards are applied when delivering criticism;
- the feedback communication process is fair – that is, the person offering feedback pays careful attention to the member of staff's ideas, shows them respect and continues to provide support despite potential disagreements.

Measuring performance

It is often said that 'what gets measured gets done' and that 'if you can't measure it you can't manage it'. For these two reasons, perhaps, the measurement of performance has come into vogue with many aspects of performance being identified as worthy of measurement. The proponents of performance measurement[32] state that measures should be relevant, significant and comprehensive. However, in following this counsel of perfection, a number of pitfalls may be encountered. For example:

- too many measures or conflicting measures may be created so that the resulting complexity cannot easily be understood or managed;

- measurement of performance is seen as an exact science rather than an art form where opinions, judgements and trade-offs are as important as gradings;
- not everything that is measurable is worth measuring or is relevant to achieving successful outcomes (for example, time-on-task in some contexts);
- some important components of successful performance are difficult to measure but still add considerable value to life at work (for example, inspirational leadership or high levels of motivation);
- in some cases it may be difficult to collect data to support the measurement process;
- since performance is itself a composite of behaviour and results, a family of linked measures is likely to be needed to measure effective performance.

Performance measurement is claimed as a useful and necessary part of HE management, given the environmental conditions in which institutions find themselves. However, we should remain properly sceptical of such claims, while experimenting with the concept and its procedures, as befits a sector committed to 'honest inquiry'. The words of Robert McNamara, ex-US Secretary of State for Defense, are worth recording:[33]

The first step is to measure whatever can be easily measured. This is OK as far as it goes. The second step is to disregard that which can't be easily measured or to give it an arbitrary quantitative value. This is artificial and misleading. The third step is to presume that what can't be measured easily really isn't important. This is blindness. The fourth step is to say that what can't be measured really doesn't exist. This is suicide.

Conclusion ∎

In this chapter we have ranged widely from the national, regional and international performance context in HE, through the concept of 'managing for performance', to the specifics of performance management systems. We have noted the value of performance management as well as the pitfalls involved in managing for performance and the dangers inherent in excessive emphasis on measurement in an area that is more an art than an exact science. HE institutions will need to explore the concept and practice of managing for performance, testing the ideas in practice and remaining ready to adjust the theory to practical realities. Evidence from other sectors suggests that good systems and procedures, when accompanied by effective leadership and management practice, will enhance performance. One without the other will not produce the same effects.

5

MANAGING TRICKY
SITUATIONS

Introduction

In an ideal world, the right people are always recruited to the right
posts, they are always well motivated and relations are always har-
monious. Unfortunately, in the real world this seldom happens and,
from time to time, tricky situations will crop up. Those that have the
potential to cause the most problems are not, surprisingly, the obvious ones. The majority of people would know the appropriate
response if, for example, someone punched the vice-chancellor on
the nose or defrauded the organization of several thousands of
pounds. No, the situations that often prove to be the most damaging
to the morale of a department or the credibility of a manager are those
that are only dealt with once they have become too big to ignore but
which, if dealt with at an earlier stage, would probably have been self-
limiting. These may be the result of deliberate mischief or unwitting
incompetence, or arise from tensions between members of the team.
However, sometimes situations arise through nobody's fault – for
example, long-term illness or disability – which require sympathetic
handling, but which are outside the experience of many managers in
HE.
    In this chapter, the following difficult situations, which often cause
managers to have sleepless nights, are examined, and some practical
advice offered:

* sickness (both long-term and short-term but recurrent);
* disability arising during the course of employment;
* drugs/alcohol problems;
* mental health problems;

- stress;
- discipline (including misuse of IT facilities);
- grievances;
- harassment and bullying.

Sickness ∎

The public sector in general, and HE in particular, is relatively new to the process of monitoring rates of sick leave, especially in relation to academic staff, but as staffing levels have become tighter, the cumulative effect on a department's performance of even average rates of sickness absence has become more significant. A survey conducted by the CIPD in 2002 of employee absence[1] revealed that the average rate of sickness absence among responding organizations was 4.4 per cent of working time, or ten working days per employee in one year. The rate for those respondents from the education sector matched the mean exactly. An estimate of the average cost of sickness absence per employee[2] among the respondents from the education sector was £608 per year. This might not seem an excessive figure, but multiplied across a whole department of, say, 30 people, the amount of money spent on sickness absence would go some way to paying the salary of an extra member of staff. Also, estimates of the cost of sickness absence tend not to take account of the impact on the morale of those expected to cover for absent colleagues, or on the ability of a group to work as a team when one or more of the members is absent.

Everyone falls sick, or has an accident, from time to time. It would, therefore, be unrealistic to expect that sickness absence could be eliminated completely, even in the best-managed organization. However, the simple act of monitoring sickness absence has been shown to reduce rates[3] and, by actively managing short- and long-term sickness absences consistently, as discussed below, further reductions can be achieved. Managing sickness absence is *not* about sacking people – the aim should be to reduce both the number of occasions staff are absent from work due to sickness and the total amount of time spent 'on the sick'.

Short-term sickness absences

In the 2002 CIPD survey of employee absence, 57 per cent of all absences were short-term (that is, less than five days). Minor illnesses, such as colds and flu, accounted for the majority of these absences. In most cases, the only management intervention necessary is to discourage staff from returning to work too soon – either while they are still infectious, or while insufficiently recovered, so that they suffer a relapse and delay their return to full fitness (and productivity). However, where short-term absences due to ill health are frequent, and particularly if a regular pattern emerges (for example, the absences tend to be on a Monday), then further investigation is warranted. First, compare the member of staff's sickness record with the departmental average – to ensure that there is genuine cause for concern. Second, review the evidence – look at the reasons for absence given on the member of staff's self-certification form over, say, the last year. This may suggest an underlying chronic medical condition, or conversely an assortment of unrelated minor ailments. Third, consult the employee. What happens next depends on your assessment of the situation. The possible reasons for short-term recurrent absences are many and various, and most are genuine. A few examples are given in Box 5.1. If you remain unconvinced that the reasons for the absences

---

Box 5.1   Recurrent short-term absences – some possible causes

- The employee may disclose emotional or family problems – you may be able to help by agreeing flexible working arrangements with them for a specified period, or by agreeing to a period of leave of absence (either paid or unpaid).
- They may be experiencing difficulties in their relationship with a colleague, or their line manager, and you may have to act as a facilitator to bring problems out into the open and agree a way forward.
- They may admit to having problems with drugs or alcohol, in which case you should encourage them to contact the institution's staff welfare service/staff counsellor/occupational health service for possible referral to appropriate support services. You should also consult your institution's policy on drug and alcohol misuse, which will provide you with a framework to manage the situation. See also the section on drug/alcohol problems (pages 105–106).
- They may have a chronic medical condition which does not significantly impair their life on a daily basis, but which does result in more sickness absence than normal. In cases such as this, you may have to accept that there is nothing you, or they, can do to reduce the amount of sickness absence, but you should work with the member of staff to develop strategies which minimize the impact of their absences on other colleagues and the effectiveness of the department.

are genuine, or if the number of absences remains unacceptably high even when steps have been taken to address the cause(s), you should inform the member of staff that you will continue to monitor their absences and, if there is no improvement over the next, say, three months, you will take further action. This may take the form of disincentives; for example, a prohibition on taking holiday until the sickness absence rate improves or requiring the member of staff to produce a doctor's certificate for every sickness absence (this is not popular with GPs and can, therefore, be very effective); or it may be formal disciplinary action. For advice on the latter, see the section on discipline (pages 114–121).

Long-term sickness absence

'Long-term' sickness absence is a shorthand expression, generally meaning the length of sickness absence that will trigger some sort of formal response by the employer, be it the involvement of the personnel/HR department, or a referral to the organization's occupational health physician. The point at which an absence becomes long term varies from employer to employer. Some organizations in the manufacturing and commercial sectors regard as long term any absence in excess of a fortnight. In the public sector, absences must generally exceed a month or more before they are regarded as long term. Your institution will probably have a sickness absence policy which will specify the point at which an absence is regarded as long term. In the absence of a formal policy, the point is normally reached when a member of staff exhausts their entitlement to sick leave on full pay (although in schemes where entitlement increases with service, this point can be reached very rapidly for relatively new staff). It is important that you adhere to the institution's policy on sickness absence, to ensure equity of treatment of staff both within and between different parts of the organization.

It is also important to seek advice from your personnel/HR department when it becomes apparent that a member of staff has been, or is likely to be, absent for an extended period. It is in the interests of the department, the institution and the member of staff to work together for a return to effective work, if at all possible, and the personnel/HR department will be able to assist in this. However, if a return to effective work is impossible, they will help to steer a safe route through the hazards of an ill health dismissal (see Chapter 7, page 172). It will almost certainly be the responsibility of the personnel/HR department to liaise with the institution's occupational physician in order to obtain independent medical advice regarding fitness to return to work, possible return date and any adjustments that might be required to facilitate a return.

One of the most important contributions that a line manager can make to the management of a long-term absence is to keep in touch with the member of staff, either directly or through colleagues. This does require the exercise of sensitivity and judgement. It is important that the member of staff feels cared for, but not put under pressure to return before they are fully fit. It is particularly important to keep contacts at the level of 'touching base' if the member of staff is absent as a result of stress, depression or anxiety, and to respect any requests that there should be no contact with work.

At one or more points during the absence a review meeting will be convened to discuss progress, a likely timeframe for return and to explore any adjustments that may be needed, either in terms of the hours of work, the working conditions or the work itself. It is important not just to inform the member of staff of their entitlements and the process being followed but also to listen to their concerns and opinions about what they feel would be best for them. It is not uncommon for a representative of the personnel/HR department to mediate review meetings, and the member of staff should be offered the option of being accompanied by a family member or friend for moral support.

It doesn't take very long away from work for someone to lose confidence in their ability to do their job. The return to work process should therefore be planned, and discussed with the member of staff in advance. Depending on the length of the absence, and the nature of the work, you may wish to propose a period of working from home, followed by a period of part-time working, building up to full hours over a period of time. You may also need to consider a short programme of refamiliarization with the more technical aspects of some jobs, if not retraining. Give some thought, also, to the social aspects of reintegrating the member of staff into the team. If they have been away for a considerable time, colleagues will have got used to not having them around, and the dynamics of the team may well have changed. It is helpful to think about this in advance and to address some of the obvious issues (for example, preparing the member of staff to meet new colleagues, or old colleagues in new roles) and so diffuse some of the early tensions.

Disability arising during the course of employment

The Disability Discrimination Act 1995 (DDA) is intended to eliminate unfair discrimination against people with disabilities. The idea is that a person's disability should not be a bar to employment unless it would significantly interfere with their ability to do the job, and there are no adjustments that the employer could be reasonably expected to make (to the working environment, to the way the work is done, to hours of work and so on).

A disabled person under the DDA is anyone 'with a physical or mental impairment which has a substantial and long-term adverse effect on his [sic] ability to carry out normal day-to-day activities'.

The employment provisions of the DDA have been in force since 1996. The Act applies both to job applicants and to existing employees, who have the right to seek assistance to retain their jobs. The UK has a particularly poor record in preventing the loss of jobs through disability or ill health. A Trades Union Congress (TUC) report[4] found that 10 per cent of victims of serious accidents return to work, compared with 50 per cent in Sweden. While the DDA does not provide absolute protection for disabled workers (the employer is only required to make *reasonable* adjustments) it does mean that employees who become disabled through the course of their employment will no longer be dismissed with not a thought given to how they might be retained. Given that employment tribunals can order unlimited awards in cases where disability discrimination is found, and that the average award in 2000 was £13,000,[5] the penalties for dismissing out of hand an employee who becomes disabled are heavy. There are also considerable benefits to be gained from making adjustments to retain a member of staff with a disability: valuable skills are retained in the organization and recruitment costs are avoided. Lloyds TSB uses a disability consultant to provide expert advice on reasonable adjustments. By the summer of 2002, the consultant had advised on more than 400 cases, achieving a retention rate of 76 per cent.[6]

Advice given by the Disability Rights Commission on what to do if a member of staff becomes disabled is given in Box 5.2. However, remember that you will not be expected to deal with the situation on your own, and that advice and support will be available from the personnel/HR department and from your institution's occupational health service.

It may be that, after a temporary period of adjustment, either to the hours of work, the tasks undertaken or the working environment, that the disabled member of staff will be able to make a full return to their job. However, in other cases, permanent adjustments may be necessary. These need not be costly, and many will actually benefit everyone. Box 5.3 lists some of the adjustments that the Disability Rights Commission suggest that employers consider.

Box 5.2   What to do if a member of staff becomes disabled

- Don't make assumptions about what the member of staff will, or will not, be able to do
- Talk to the person about what they think the effect of their disability will be
- Consider whether to seek specialist advice (from disability employment advisers, the rehabilitation service of relevant charities, or from consultants)
- Consult other employees, having first sought the permission of the disabled person
- Look again at the job description and person specification – is it accurate, can some tasks be done differently, are required elements really necessary?
- Be fair – a disabled person should not be expected to perform at a higher level than someone without a disability
- Put yourself in the disabled person's shoes – how would you wish to be treated?

Box 5.3   Possible adjustments to enable a person with a disability to return to work

---

- Adjustments to the workplace (for example, lowering light switches so that they are accessible to someone in a wheelchair; improving access routes; redecoration to improve contrast so that people with a visual impairment can navigate more easily)
- Adjustments to the job (reallocation of minor duties to another member of staff; provision of additional supervision, if appropriate; redeployment; relocation; allowing working from home)
- Adjustments to working hours (reduction to part-time hours; flexibility in working hours, for example, to fit in with the availability of a carer or to avoid the rush hour; allowing absences during working hours, for example, for rehabilitation, assessment or treatment)
- Provision of additional/appropriate training (for example, for a visually impaired person to learn how to use voice operated software)
- Provision of specialist equipment and/or support (for example, a telephone with text display for a deaf person; providing Braille or large print versions of written material; providing a reader or interpreter)

Drugs/alcohol problems   ■

Under the Health and Safety at Work Act 1974, a university or college has a duty to ensure the health and safety of staff, students and visitors. The risks to health and safety will increase if a member of staff's performance is impaired by the consumption of drugs and alcohol, and a number of universities have adopted drugs and alcohol policies in recent years.[7] The misuse of alcohol and drugs has also been demonstrated to increase absenteeism,[8] reduce productivity and damage team morale and employee relations, so there are many good reasons for not ignoring the impact of drugs and alcohol in the workplace.

In certain contexts – for example, driving, operating machinery or working in a laboratory (especially if working with organic solvents) – the potential consequences of impaired performance due to alcohol or drugs are obvious. In such 'safety critical' jobs, being under the influence may be an immediate disciplinary offence. It is important that staff involved in safety critical work are reminded of the potential effects on their performance of drinking, not only during the working day but also out of working hours.[9] Similar considerations also apply to those whose jobs require them to be 'on call'. Any member of staff who is unexpectedly called into work and who feels that their judgement may be impaired should discuss this with the senior manager in charge and a decision taken as to whether they are fit to continue. The potential impact of impaired performance in other jobs should not be ignored. For example, students may suffer from poor quality lecturing or inadequate supervision which could have a detrimental affect on their performance.

Dependency on drugs or alcohol should be regarded as a medical condition, and disciplinary action only taken as a last resort. The Health and Safety Executive (HSE) publication, *Don't Mix It! – A Guide for Employers on Alcohol at Work*,[10] points out that a dismissal may be found to be unfair if an employer has made no attempt to help an employee whose problems at work are due to alcohol dependence. Staff who believe that they may have an alcohol or drugs related problem should be advised to seek appropriate professional help (for example, from their GP, a specialist alcohol/drugs agency or counselling service) and reasonable absences for advice, counselling or treatment should be regarded as normal sick leave. It may be necessary to consider a temporary transfer to other duties during treatment if the dependency means that there is an increased risk to the member of staff or others. It would, however, be appropriate to consider invoking disciplinary action in the following circumstances:

- if help with an alcohol or drug related problem is refused and poor performance or conduct continues;
- if treatment is unreasonably discontinued or if, after a reasonable period of time, there is no improvement in behaviour or work performance remains poor (however, it is important to recognize that recovery from alcohol or drugs dependency can take some time and that relapses may occur);
- gross misconduct while under the influence of alcohol or drugs;
- illegal possession, use or supply of controlled drugs[11] while at work.

It can be very difficult for someone to admit to themselves, let alone others, that they have an alcohol or drug related problem. Signs that an alcohol or drug problem may be present are given in Box 5.4.

It is not only illegal drugs that can impair work performance. Some prescribed drugs (for example, some antidepressants) and over-the-counter medicines (for example, cold/flu remedies and antihistamines) can also have adverse effects on performance. Staff taking such medicines should be encouraged to discuss this with their line manager or supervisor so that appropriate modifications to their work or working environment may be put in place.

Mental health problems

Discrimination against people who suffer, or who have suffered, from mental illness is still common in western societies, and particularly in the workplace. Unfair treatment of those who most need support is the result of ignorance, fear or both, despite the fact that one in four people will experience some form of mental health problem during the course of a year. Mental health problems affect people in a host of different ways and many may need little or no support at work. Such is the stigma attached to mental illness that many people are

---

Box 5.4 Alcohol or drug related problems – signs to look for[12]

- Slurred speech, unsteady gait etc.
- Sudden mood changes
- Unusual irritability or aggression
- Unusual fluctuations in concentration or energy
- Impaired work performance and timekeeping
- Deterioration in relationships with colleagues
- Dishonesty, theft etc.

reluctant to disclose a condition affecting their mental health if this can be avoided.

The HSE recommends that organizations should incorporate mental health into their health and safety at work policies. Also, mental illness may be covered by the DDA, affording a degree of protection to sufferers against unfair discrimination in employment. It is important, therefore, that managers are aware of mental health issues in relation to employment, from ensuring that job descriptions and person specifications are drawn up in a way that will enable adjustments to be made to accommodate people with a mental health problem to understanding the effect of workplace stress on the mental health of staff (see the following section on stress, pages 109–114).

The two examples in Box 5.5 illustrate (i) the dangers of overlooking the DDA in relation to mental illness and getting things wrong, and (ii) taking the DDA fully into account, and getting things right.

One situation in which both managers and staff can feel particularly anxious is the return to work of an employee after a long absence due to a mental health problem. Although rehabilitation after a mental health problem will usually be more cost effective than early retirement, the employee will have concerns not only about their competence but also about their relationships with colleagues. Colleagues may find it difficult to rebuild their relationship with a returning team member and the manager will be hoping for the best but probably fearing the worst. The keys to steering all parties through a potentially uncomfortable period are preparation and

---

Box 5.5   Importance of the DDA in relation to mental illness – examples

Example 1: getting it wrong[13]

Mr G was a paranoid schizophrenic, who misinterpreted the words and actions of others, suffered from auditory hallucinations that caused him to leave the office and suffered poor concentration. He was sacked following complaints from colleagues. The EAT found that the DDA applied and that he had been unfairly dismissed.

Example 2: getting it right

An employee of Hampshire County Council felt anxious in team settings and would not communicate with colleagues, yet was very effective at doing her job. The council provided her with email, voicemail and homeworking facilities.

Box 5.6   The importance of careful monitoring following a return to work[14]

Mr Y took four months off work because of depression. He returned to work on a flexible basis, whereby he could attend or not as he pleased, take breaks when he needed to and was not required to do any work if he didn't feel able to. However, he was back at work for only seven weeks before he went off sick again with a recurrence of his depression. Despite the arrangements for flexible working that were put in place after his first absence, it was found that during the seven weeks following his return he went on a week-long residential training course, which he found very stressful, and provided holiday cover for the workshop manager. On the manager's return, pressure of work meant that Mr Y was left to run the workshop. Mr Y did not tell his employer at any time that he felt unable to cope – indeed, he believed he could cope. However, the Court of Appeal found that a recurrence of Mr Y's condition was foreseeable, if appropriate action was not taken on his return to work. Had Mr Y's employers implemented the arrangements that had been agreed with regard to flexible working when he returned, then the recurrence may well have been avoided, but the employers failed to monitor Mr Y's situation and were in breach of their duty of care to him.

Box 5.7   Preparing for a return to work

- If possible, maintain contact with the employee while they are away and particularly in the period leading up to the return so that adjustments can be made
- Provide appropriate information for colleagues, drawing on professional advice as necessary
- Use the return to work interview to determine whether all necessary adjustments have been made
- Use follow-up meetings to monitor progress for at least six months after return to work
- Ensure effective, ongoing liaison between the employee, line manager and specialists as required
- Employees should be viewed as vulnerable and any changes to their duties should be monitored

communication. The example in Box 5.6 demonstrates the importance of careful monitoring once someone has returned to work.

Box 5.7 includes some advice on preparing for a return to work.

Stress ∎

The HSE defines stress as: 'the adverse reaction people have to excessive pressure or other types of demand placed on them'.[15] Pressure is
sometimes beneficial and people can respond positively to deadlines
and targets, finding in them an opportunity for growth and development. This positive pressure is sometimes described as 'healthy stress'.
However, when pressure becomes excessive, people begin to respond
negatively. This 'unhealthy stress' can result in a range of physical
and psychological symptoms including:

- mental health problems (including anxiety, depression and panic
  attacks);
- heart disease;
- back pain;
- gastrointestinal problems;
- minor health problems such as gum disease, shortness of breath,
  dizziness, earache, headache, chest pains and dermatitis.

The 2002 CIPD survey of employee absence revealed that stress was
the most significant reason for long-term absence (that is, longer than
four weeks) among non-manual workers, particularly in the public
sector. In 1996, the Institute of Management estimated that every day
270,000 people take time off work because of work-related stress, at a
cost of some £7 billion a year. In individual workplaces, sickness
absence due to the effects of stress can have a domino effect – if the
workload of an absent colleague is simply shared out among those
staff who are left, the increased pressure may, in time, have an adverse
effect on their health. There are, therefore, powerful financial and
organizational reasons to try to reduce the amount of unhealthy
stress to which members of staff are exposed. In addition, there are
legal duties that employers owe to their employees – namely, to
provide a safe working environment and the common law 'duty of
care'. The landmark case is that of *Walker* v. *Northumberland County
Council*,[16] which is described in Box 5.8.

It is important to remember that the ability to cope with stress not
only varies between individuals, but even in the same individual over
time. There are many causes of unhealthy stress, not all of them
connected with the workplace (it is well documented that the life

---

Box 5.8 *Walker v. Northumberland County Council*

Mr Walker suffered a nervous breakdown, due to overwork, after 17 years with the council. He returned to work after six months, with additional assistance, but with no other adjustments to his duties or workload. However, the assistance was withdrawn after a month, as he seemed to be 'coping'. He suffered a second nervous breakdown shortly thereafter. It was found that, while the employers could not be held liable for the first breakdown, they had failed in their duty of care by not making adequate adjustments to Mr Walker's workload, having been alerted to the difficulties he was experiencing. Mr Walker was awarded damages of £170,000, but the total cost to the council (including sick pay, ill health pension costs and legal expenses) was more than double that sum.

Box 5.9 Causes of stress in the workplace

Work practices

- Lack of control – of job content or ways of working
- Lack of a clear job description or lines of responsibility
- Uncertainty – about job security or career prospects
- Long hours culture
- Lack of recognition – of good performance
- No opportunity to voice concerns
- Too much work or inadequate time in which to do the job to required standards
- Too little work, or work that is insufficiently challenging
- Too much responsibility coupled with too little authority
- Unsupportive, unsympathetic (or worse) line management

Relationships

- Prolonged conflict between individuals
- Harassment or bullying
- Discrimination

Environment and technology

- Unpleasant or hazardous working conditions
- Intrusive technology that reduces workers' control of the job

experiences people find most stressful are bereavement, moving house and divorce). However, stress is cumulative, and it may be that an individual is able to cope with a very stressful event in their personal life, providing that the pressures in their working life are not excessive. Nor does stress in the workplace arise just from excessive workloads (although that is the most obvious cause). Some of the causes of stress at work are set out in Box 5.9.

People sometimes fail to recognize when they are beginning to suffer the effects of unhealthy stress, and will either ignore their symptoms, or blame them on something else. Others will be aware that they are under excessive pressure, but will be unwilling, or feel unable, to either do anything about it, or to ask for help. If ignored, the symptoms of unhealthy stress can result in serious physical or psychological damage. It is in everyone's interests for managers to be able to recognize the symptoms in their colleagues and so be able to intervene before problems become serious. Table 5.1 sets out some of the more common symptoms of unhealthy stress.

If you believe a member of staff is showing signs of unhealthy stress, don't hide your head under the metaphorical blankets in the hope that the problem will go away, tempting though that may be. Talk to them and encourage them to work with you to identify the

Table 5.1 Recognizing the symptoms of unhealthy stress

Behavioural symptoms	Increased sickness absence
	Mood swings
	Apathy
	Increased use of tobacco/alcohol/drugs
	Indecision
	Increased incidence of accidents
	Evading duties and responsibilities
	Complaining
Emotional symptoms	Anxiety
	Irritability
	Low self-esteem and confidence
	Depression
	Aggression
	Withdrawal from social contact
Organizational symptoms	Reduced staff morale
	Resistance to change
	Poor staff performance
	Poor staff retention rate
	Increased absenteeism

Table 5.2 Tackling unhealthy stress – some suggestions

Source of unhealthy stress	Possible solution
Workloads and deadlines	Use regular appraisals and reviews of workload. Consider worksharing, reorganization of tasks and training to address excessive workloads and unrealistic deadlines
Change	Ensure that change is managed and that the need for change and the change process are communicated to staff regularly. Ensure that the impact of change is equitable, and seen to be so
Control, responsibility and autonomy	Ensure that job descriptions and management lines are accurate and apparent. Ensure that supervision is appropriate to the task and the individual working style. Ensure that staff feel able to voice concerns about what they are expected to do and how they are expected to do it
Working relationships	Investigate allegations of harassment or bullying thoroughly and take action as appropriate (see pages 123–129). Genuine personality clashes may have to be resolved by moving one or both of the parties involved
Working conditions and environment	Where possible, address any physical aspects of the working environment that have a negative impact on well-being. Keep the working environment under review – small irritations can become big issues and, conversely, small improvements can make a big difference to morale

biggest sources of stress. Where possible, remove the source of the stress (Table 5.2 gives some suggestions to address some common causes of unhealthy stress).

If removing the source of unhealthy stress is not possible, work with the member of staff to reduce harmful effects (for example, by developing different ways of working, by changing some aspect of the working environment, or by coming to accept that it isn't necessary for every task to be completed perfectly and that 'good enough' will do). If the major source of unhealthy stress is in the member of staff's personal life rather than at work, investigate if more flexible working hours or some other kind of support would help. If your institution

Box 5.10	What to do if an employee is showing signs of unhealthy stress – a checklist

- Don't ignore it!
- Talk to the member of staff
- Carry out a risk assessment to identify source(s) of stress
- Remove causes of stress, if possible, or take action to reduce effects, if not
- Monitor the situation and review actions as necessary
- Seek advice from personnel/HR or occupational health if problems persist

offers support in the form of staff counselling or an employee assistance programme, draw this to the attention of the member of staff. The personnel/HR department will almost certainly be happy to talk to individual staff on an entirely confidential basis, too. Monitor the situation, and review the actions taken if unhealthy stress begins to be a problem again. What to do if an employee is showing signs of unhealthy stress is summarized in Box 5.10.

Sometimes, particularly with small, close-knit groups, whole teams will show symptoms of unhealthy stress. There will be a lot of moaning and complaining, short-term absences will increase, even for those staff whose absence records had previously been good, there will be a reluctance to accept change, even if it is self-evidently for the better, staff will be demoralized and dissatisfied and often unable to see a way of things ever improving, team spirit will be next to nonexistent as staff try to protect themselves. Positive steps must be taken if the team is not to become locked into a vicious downward cycle. Often the pressures leading to the unhealthy stress are beyond the control of the team or department (for example, chronic underresourcing, rapid unmanaged change imposed from outside). In these circumstances, it can be helpful to look at ways of making small improvements, to help the team regain a sense of control. It may also be helpful to arrange an externally facilitated 'awayday' for the team so that unspoken tensions within the team can be brought out into the open and addressed, and the foundations laid for a consensus on the way forward. Some other practical suggestions to address unhealthy stress in teams are given in Box 5.11.

Information relevant to managing stress may also be found later in this chapter (page 128. See also Chapter 6).

Box 5.11 Practical steps to address unhealthy stress in teams

- Improve communication flows – both upwards and downwards (introduce team meetings where everyone feels able to contribute; circulate time-sensitive information by email to the whole team; consult *meaningfully*)
- Develop a culture of continuous process review – encourage every team member to look at what they do and to suggest improvements for streamlining – and act on good suggestions
- Give praise where praise is due – publicly if appropriate
- Promote collaboration within the team, not competition
- Don't expect the team to cover for absent colleagues indefinitely – bring in support as soon as practicable
- Address conflicts within the team at the earliest opportunity – they won't go away if you ignore them
- Tackle poor performance within the context of fair and transparent procedures – no one likes to carry passengers, but no one wants to be picked on, either
- Encourage people to take their holiday entitlement
- Discourage people from working excessive hours on a regular basis
- Take a good look at yourself as a manager – ask others for feedback on your management style and take steps to address any problems identified

---

Discipline

Why disciplinary rules and procedures are important

In all but the very smallest organizations there is a need for rules to govern the behaviour of employees while at work, and also for procedures to be used when conduct or performance fails to meet acceptable standards. The aim of these procedures should not be to provide a justification for the punishment of offenders, but to help and encourage all employees to achieve and maintain the required standards while ensuring fair and consistent treatment for everyone. The areas covered by disciplinary rules will vary with the needs and culture of the organization, but will typically include timekeeping, absenteeism, health and safety, use of the organization's facilities (personal telephone calls, use of stationery and so on), discrimination and gross misconduct.

Many managers, particularly those in academic departments, are often reluctant to act on relatively minor shortcomings in conduct or performance, out of fear of causing friction in close working relationships. However, failure to address minor problems early on, perhaps with no more than a gentle rebuke, has the potential to create bigger difficulties later:

- when action is finally taken it may well come as a surprise to the employee, who will resent not having been given an opportunity to address their shortcomings at an earlier stage;
- a *laissez-faire* climate may be created which will make more strict enforcement that much harder to achieve;
- infringements that are regularly overlooked will compromise management credibility among staff who see their colleagues 'getting away' with poor performance or unacceptable behaviour.

The law requires employers to have a minimum, three-step, formal disciplinary procedure, as set out in Box 5.12.

It is very important that disciplinary procedures are followed fairly and consistently, even for minor offences – many employers have had tribunal claims decided against them on procedural grounds alone. The Employment Act 2002 provides that failure to complete the minimum disciplinary procedure set out above will render a dismissal automatically unfair (see Chapter 7, pages 168–173 for advice on how to handle dismissals fairly).

In the chartered universities, the Model Statute specifies disciplinary procedures for academic staff. In January 2003, the Privy Council approved a draft revised statute, which institutions could choose to incorporate into their own statutes. As well as specifying the circumstances in which disciplinary action could be taken and requiring institutions to adopt ordinances in order to promulgate disciplinary procedures to deal with less serious matters, the draft revised statute also set out the penalties which may be applied as a result of disciplinary action. In addition to warnings and dismissal, these include, for staff appointed or promoted after the statute comes into effect, the withholding of salary increments, suspension without pay for up to three months and demotion and/or loss of title.

The Model Statute does not apply to academic staff in incorporated universities or colleges of HE. In these institutions, the board of governors determines disciplinary procedures for all staff and it is more likely that a single procedure will apply.

Box 5.12 Statutory minimum disciplinary procedure (Employment Act 2002)

Step 1: statement of the offence

- The employer must set out in writing the employee's alleged offence (by way of conduct, performance or otherwise) which has caused the employer to contemplate taking disciplinary action and give the statement, or a copy, to the employee

Step 2: the meeting

- The employer must invite the employee to a meeting to discuss the matter
- The meeting must take place before any action (other than suspension) is taken, but after the employer has notified the employee of the grounds for the meeting and the employee has had a reasonable opportunity to consider their response
- The employee must take all reasonable steps to attend the meeting
- After the meeting, the employer must inform the employee of their final decision and advise the employee of their right to appeal if they are dissatisfied with the decision

Step 3: the appeal

- The employee must inform the employer if they wish to appeal
- The employer must invite the employee to a further meeting
- The employee must take all reasonable steps to attend the meeting
- After the meeting, the employer must inform the employee of their final decision

General requirements

- All steps must be taken without unreasonable delay
- The timing and location of meetings must be reasonable
- Meetings must be conducted in such a way that both sides can put their case
- Wherever possible, appeal meetings should be conducted by a more senior manager than the manager involved in the original decision

The normal disciplinary standards should apply to trade union officials just as they do to other employees. However, no action should be taken against such an official beyond an oral warning without first discussing all the circumstances of the case with a senior trade union representative or full-time official. This is to avoid the disciplinary action being construed as an attack on the union's functions.

Disciplinary procedures in practice

The penalties imposed when disciplinary action is taken will typically include warnings, demotion, transfer, suspension without pay, or, ultimately, dismissal. However, the penalty must be proportionate to the offence. A tribunal would not consider it reasonable to dismiss someone for being late on a couple of occasions and the Advisory, Concilliation and Arbitration Service (ACAS) code of practice, *Disciplinary Practice and Procedures in Employment*, stipulates that employees should not be dismissed for the first breach of discipline, except in the case of gross misconduct. The penalty must also be permitted under the terms of the contract of employment (fining an employee for persistent lateness may seem a good idea, but if the contract of employment doesn't allow for such a penalty, you will not only be acting unfairly, but will also be guilty of making unlawful deductions from pay).

The formal disciplinary procedures of most organizations provide for an oral warning and two written warnings before dismissal. The warnings are intended to help the employee improve their conduct or performance and should therefore specify what improvement is expected within a defined timescale as well as spelling out the consequences of further complaints (either further warnings or dismissal). All written warnings (and a note of oral warnings) should be signed, dated and kept on record for the period specified in the disciplinary rules or procedure.

While the importance of following the correct sequence of warnings fairly and consistently cannot be overstated, it is not always appropriate if the infringement is of a serious nature. Summary dismissal will be appropriate if gross misconduct has been established while a final written warning without previous warnings will be appropriate in the case of serious misconduct short of gross misconduct. Some examples of gross misconduct are given in Box 5.13.

A growing area of concern with regard to misconduct is that of computer misuse. Organizations are encouraged to have clear,

---

Box 5.13 Examples of gross misconduct

- Pilferage and theft
- Fraud (including falsification of timesheets)
- Physical assault
- Malicious damage to equipment or colleagues'/students' property
- Negligent behaviour endangering a colleague's/student's life
- Submission of false references

Box 5.14 Examples of computer misuse

- Inappropriate use of email that interferes with others' legitimate use of computer services or may constitute harassment
- Unauthorized commercial work for outside bodies
- Attempting to access the username or password of another user
- Masquerading as another user
- Deliberate viewing and/or printing of pornographic images
- Distribution of obscene, offensive or abusive material
- Unauthorized interference with information belonging to another person

---

well-publicized guidelines on what is and is not considered appropriate use of email, internet and other computer facilities and most HEIs have these. Box 5.14 gives some examples of the most common forms of computer misuse. If computer misuse is suspected, this should be reported to an appropriate person in the institution's computer centre (or equivalent).

It will not be appropriate to invoke the disciplinary procedure in every case of poor performance or misconduct. For example, if poor attendance due to sickness is giving cause for concern and investigation reveals a genuine underlying medical problem, consideration should be given to what support the organization can provide while the problem is being resolved. If the problem cannot be resolved within a reasonable time, transfer to a less demanding job or dismissal on the grounds of ill health might be appropriate (see Chapter 7, pages 172–173). If an employee's conduct with colleagues or students has deteriorated, investigation may reveal problems in their personal life. In these circumstances, the member of staff should be advised of appropriate sources of help both within and outside the institution, and consideration given to whether leave of absence, or temporary adjustments to their hours of work might be helpful (see Chapter 6 for advice on the various statutory forms of leave available for the care of dependants, including children, and also on flexible working options).

Implementing a disciplinary procedure

The investigation

When a possible breach of discipline has come to the notice of managers, the first step should be to investigate the case, suspending the employee on full pay if necessary in the case of serious misconduct. The investigation may include collecting witness statements, gathering documents and analysing records. If it is necessary to interview the employee it should be made clear that the purpose of the interview is purely to gather factual information and that it does not form part of the disciplinary process.

The invitation to the hearing

Investigation may reveal that the situation has arisen from a failure in management or that further training is needed – in these cases disciplinary action would be inappropriate. If it is decided that disciplinary action is appropriate, the employee should be informed in writing of the complaint against them and invited to attend a disciplinary interview. They should be given sufficient time to prepare their response and to arrange for witnesses to be called if they wish, and they should be informed of their right to be accompanied by a colleague or trade union official. You may wish to encourage them to be accompanied, as the presence of a companion often means that the interview can be conducted much more smoothly, in part because an accompanied employee is less likely to succumb to feelings of paranoia and in part because an objective representative can discourage any unrealistic expectations the employee may have. The presence of a colleague or representative also lessens the scope for later disagreement about what was actually discussed.

The hearing

Ideally, the head of department should chair the meeting with the employee's line manager presenting the case against the employee and a representative of personnel/HR present to advise and keep notes. If this is not practicable the manager holding the interview should arrange for at least one other person to assist, remembering not to involve anyone who may be involved in a subsequent appeal.

The interview should follow a systematic and fair sequence, as it should be neither an interrogation nor an informal chat. The manager in the chair should explain the purpose of the meeting, who everyone is and why they are there, and how the interview is to be conducted. The line manager should then set out the complaint against the employee together with the facts supporting the decision to hold the interview. If witnesses are called, the employee or their representative should have an opportunity to question them about their statements. The employee or their representative should then be invited to respond, calling witnesses if they wish, whom management may question.

Having allowed an opportunity for closing remarks and clarification of any points still at issue, the manager in the chair should summarize what has been heard and adjourn the meeting for a decision to be taken or, if necessary, for further investigation of any new information presented at the meeting. This adjournment is important even in apparently straightforward cases because the employee must feel that they have had a fair opportunity to state their case and that what they have said has been taken into account before a decision is reached.

The outcome

During the adjournment, management should consider carefully all the information that has been presented, taking into account the employee's previous disciplinary record and any current warnings, before reaching their decision. The meeting should be reconvened for the chair to announce the decision, and to remind the employee of their right of appeal. The outcome of the meeting should then be confirmed in writing to the employee and a copy kept on record for the period specified in the procedure.

Appeals

The disciplinary procedure should set out the time limit for lodging an appeal, what form the appeal statement should take and who is responsible for hearing any appeal. A higher level of management should hear appeals than that which authorized the disciplinary action and it is vital to ensure that no one involved in the original decision is a party to the appeal, except as a witness.

Box 5.15 gives a manager's checklist for implementing a disciplinary procedure.

Box 5.15   Manager's checklist for disciplinary action

- Investigate the complaint, fairly and thoroughly
- Notify the employee of the outcome of the investigation, even if you decide to take the matter no further
- Consider whether there are any special circumstances, and whether there is a need for further training, etc.
- Don't ignore minor offences; issue an informal rebuke if that is all that is required
- If there is still a case to answer, invite employee to the disciplinary interview
- Remind the employee of their right to be accompanied by a trade union official or a colleague of their choice
- At interview, ensure the employee has adequate opportunity to state their case
- Remember to adjourn the meeting to reach a decision
- Remind the employee of their right of appeal
- Confirm the decision in writing – ensure that warnings specify the improvements expected within a particular timescale and the consequences of failure to improve; keep a signed and dated copy on record
- Monitor future performance and/or conduct

Grievances

Grievances arise from time to time in all organizations over a range of issues, including terms and conditions of employment, supervision or management, conditions of work, discrimination or harassment, bullying or health and safety. The law requires employers to have a minimum, three-step, formal grievance procedure, as set out in Box 5.16.

Formal grievance procedures are typically contained in a staff handbook, conditions of service or sometimes, for academic staff in chartered universities, in the institution's statutes. In addition, there may well be other formal complaints procedures to cover the sensitive issues of harassment and bullying. Heads of department often have a key role in the early stages of the procedure and it is important that they, and other managers who may be involved in the formal process, understand their responsibilities and adhere to the requirements that are set out in the procedure, particularly with regard to time-scales and the provision of information. Employees are entitled to be

---

Box 5.16 Statutory minimum grievance procedure
(Employment Act 2002)

Step 1: statement of grievance

- The employee must set out the grievance in writing and give the statement, or a copy, to the employer

Step 2: the meeting

- The employer must invite the employee to a meeting to discuss the matter
- The employee must take all reasonable steps to attend the meeting
- After the meeting, the employer must inform the employee of their final decision and advise the employee of their right to appeal if they are dissatisfied with the decision

Step 3: the appeal

- The employee must inform the employer if they wish to appeal
- The employer must invite the employee to a further meeting
- The employee must take all reasonable steps to attend the meeting
- After the meeting, the employer must inform the employee of their final decision

General requirements

- All steps must be taken without unreasonable delay
- The timing and location of meetings must be reasonable
- Meetings must be conducted in such a way that both sides can put their case
- Wherever possible, employers should be represented at the appeal meeting by a more senior manager than the manager involved in the original decision

---

accompanied at formal grievance hearings by 'a single companion', who can be either a trade union official or a colleague.

If there is one thing guaranteed to cause a manager's heart to sink, it is being told that a member of staff in their department intends to pursue a formal grievance. The reason for this is simple – whatever the grounds for the member of staff's complaint, whether it is justified or not, there are seldom, if any, winners once the formal procedures are invoked. Even if one side or other is vindicated (and, often, the result is an unsatisfactory stalemate, with fault attributed to both sides), working relationships tend to be damaged irretrievably. Given the damage that can result from formal grievances, it is better by far to try to resolve difficulties at as early a stage as possible. This can be easier said than done, but few problems do the decent thing and go away when they are ignored. Your personnel/HR department will be able to provide support in a number of ways, from being a confidential sounding-board, to advising on strategies for implementation on the ground, to facilitating meetings between aggrieved parties. Box 5.17 gives some advice for tackling relatively small problems before they get to be big ones, and the case studies in Boxes 5.18 and 5.19 provide two examples of issues that can, but need not, escalate into formal grievances, providing there is early intervention.

Harassment and bullying

The legal context

Although harassment, as an explicit term, was not included in the SDA 1975, the RRA 1976 or the DDA 1995, employment tribunals have consistently found that behaviour that may be construed as harassment is a 'detriment' which is illegal if it is demonstrated that the complainants were subjected to it because of their sex, ethnicity or disability. There is no limit on the award a tribunal may make in discrimination cases, and some have been substantial. Legal protection against discrimination (and hence harassment) on the grounds of sexual orientation and religion came into effect in 2003, with

Box 5.17	Some hints on how to resolve little local difficulties while they are still little

- Don't be an ostrich
- Don't take sides
- Don't rely on other people being 'reasonable'
- Don't expect people to back down, just because it would be easier for you
- Do choose your time (if possible)
- Do be fair and consistent
- Do anticipate the reactions of others
- Do have plans C and D, as well as B

Box 5.18 Case study 1 – 'Always the bridesmaid, never the bride'

Professor A was coordinating her first promotions round as a newly appointed head of department. One of her colleagues, Dr B, had submitted a case for promotion to senior lecturer in each of the last two years and had received detailed feedback on the reasons for his failure to be promoted each year. He was convinced that his promotion was long overdue and had indicated that he wished to be put forward again. Professor A looked carefully at his case, and the feedback that he had been given in previous years, and concluded that he still fell some way short of the standard that the Promotions Committee would be applying. She also realized that her predecessor did not discuss Dr B's promotion case with him the previous year, although it was obvious that it was bound to fail, but 'hid behind the committee' when the inevitable happened. Professor A decided that, in fairness to Dr B, she should try to persuade him to delay seeking promotion for a further 12 months, by which time his case would be much stronger. She realized that this would not be well received so she (i) obtained anonymized information about the profiles of recently promoted candidates from cognate disciplines, (ii) arranged for the dean of the faculty to meet Dr B with her, and (iii) offered to appoint a mentor to support Dr B in the preparation of his next promotion bid. As Professor A had anticipated, Dr B was furious that his new head of department was not prepared to support his bid for promotion and complained to his union rep, with a view to pursuing a formal grievance. After discussing the case with Professor A, the rep was able to convince Dr B that his head of department was actually offering meaningful and practical support for his case rather than passively allowing him to fail as her predecessor had.

---

similar measures concerning age due to follow in 2006. Persons who feel that they have been harassed may also bring a claim under the Human Rights Act 1998, which prohibits discrimination on the grounds of sex, race, colour, language, religion, political or other opinion, national or social origin, birth, property or status. The Criminal Justice and Public Order Act 1994 defines a criminal offence of intentional harassment. A person is guilty of an offence under this Act if they use threatening, abusive or insulting words or behaviour with the intention of harassing another, or if they display written material that is threatening, abusive or insulting and causes another person to feel harassed.

Box 5.19   Case study 2 – 'A well-oiled machine?'

The general office of the Department of Miscellaneous Studies was not a happy place. It had been at one time, but a period of enforced change coinciding with rapid turnover of staff had left its mark. Demarcations between the various support staff were entrenched, cover for absences was grudging at best and working practices were inefficient. D was convinced that she had to carry a much heavier workload than E, F was constantly complaining, G hoped that by being positive and enthusiastic the others might take the hint, while H let everyone know that as the head of department's secretary, she was far too busy to help out. The departmental administrator decided that enough was enough. Following the advice of the HR department, she persuaded the head of department to allocate part of the training budget to a facilitated 'away-day' for the general office team. The event provided a forum for the staff to air their concerns about workloads, working practices and communication within the office. It gave them an opportunity to listen to and be heard by their colleagues and, overcoming initial scepticism, laid the foundations for an ongoing team-building process.

The discrimination legislation holds the employer responsible for acts of discrimination committed by employees in the course of their employment, even if the acts were unauthorized and the employer had no knowledge of them. Employment tribunals consider employers' liability routinely in harassment cases, and will look for evidence that the employer took reasonable steps to prevent harassment. In this regard, the tribunals will take account of the codes of practice for employment produced by the various discrimination commissions, in addition to European legislation and codes of practice (such as the European Commission code of practice, *Protecting the Dignity of Women and Men at Work 1991*). Universities and colleges, as public bodies, also have a duty under the Race Relations (Amendment) Act 2000 to eliminate racial discrimination.[17]

Employees who believe they have been bullied can take action against their employers under the Health and Safety at Work Act 1974 (which requires employers to ensure, as far as possible, the health, safety and welfare at work of all employees) and the Management of Health and Safety at Work Regulations 1999 (which require employers to conduct risk assessments and to take necessary action to remove or mitigate identified risks).

Harassment

The CIPD defines harassment as 'unwanted behaviour which a person finds intimidating, upsetting, embarrassing, humiliating or offensive'.[18] Sexual and racial harassment are probably the forms that come most readily to mind, but people may also be subjected to harassment on the grounds of disability, sexual orientation, age and religious or political belief (although it should be noted that, at the time of writing, there is no clear legal definition of what constitutes 'religious belief'). Table 5.3 sets out some examples of the type of behaviour that may constitute harassment.

Bullying

The CIPD defines bullying as: 'persistent behaviour directed against an individual which is intimidating, offensive or malicious and which undermines the confidence and self-esteem of the recipient'.[19] Bullying differs from harassment, as there is no apparent bias towards race, gender or disability. Research suggests that workplace bullying is very prevalent in the UK. In a study undertaken by Hoel and Cooper in 1999,[20] 5300 people responded to a questionnaire survey sent to 70 organizations in both the public and private sectors. Approximately 10 per cent of respondents reported that they had been bullied in the previous six months. Bullying appeared to be most prevalent in teaching, in the prison service and in the post and telecommunications sector, with more than 15 per cent of respondents from these sectors reporting that they had been bullied. Approximately 7 per cent of respondents from HE reported that they had been bullied.

Those who have been bullied often report feeling let down by not only their employers, but also by their unions, because line managers, personnel/HR and union officials ignore their complaints. This may explain why the UK Bullying Advice Line, set up in 1996, has found that in 90 per cent of cases the source of bullying can be traced to an individual with a history of bullying behaviour – the failure to act on complaints allows bullies to transfer their unwelcome attentions to new targets. It is important, therefore, that employers take steps to create an environment that discourages bullying and takes strong action when it is found to have occurred. However, bullies do not have the word 'Bully' tattooed across their foreheads. In many cases, they are plausible individuals who are charming with people other than those that they are bullying. The Hoel and Cooper study found that bullying was most often linked to management behaviour (in HE, 62 per cent of bullying was

Table 5.3 Examples of behaviour that may constitute harassment[21]

Type of harassment	Example of indicative behaviours
Sexual harassment (unwelcome physical, verbal or non-verbal conduct of a sexual nature)	Touching, groping, invasion of personal space, sexual assault, rape, indecent exposure Personal comments, sexual slurs, belittling, suggestive, lewd or abusive remarks, explicit 'jokes' or innuendo, sexual demands Suggestive looks, leering, explicit gestures, sexually explicit emails, display of pornographic material in the workplace
Racial harassment (unwanted behaviour based on race, ethnicity or nationality)	Derogatory name-calling, insults, racist 'jokes' and graffiti, the display of offensive insignia, ridicule based on cultural differences, verbal abuse, damage to property, threats, physical attack
Harassment on the grounds of disability (unwanted behaviour based on disability, impairment or special need)	Patronizing or objectionable comments, inappropriate references to disability, refusal to work or socialize with people with disabilities, addressing/talking to carers/notetakers/interpreters rather than to the disabled person
Harassment on the grounds of sexual orientation (unwanted behaviour based on known or presumed sexual orientation)	Derogatory comments and name-calling, stereotyping, verbal abuse, actual or threatened disclosure of sexuality, exclusion of same-sex partners from social events to which other sex partners are invited, intrusive questioning about domestic arrangements, physical assault
Harassment on the grounds of religious belief (unwanted behaviour based on religious belief or practices)	Ridiculing items worn for religious reasons, denigrating cultural customs, derisory comments regarding religious belief

committed by managers), but colleagues, subordinates and customers/students are responsible for a significant amount of bullying too. By being aware that bullying goes on, and the forms it can take, managers will be better able to respond when a complaint is made.

Box 5.20 Common forms of workplace bullying

- Verbal or physical threats
- Unjustified, persistent criticism
- Offensive or abusive personal remarks
- Setting someone up to fail (for example, setting unattainable targets, withholding necessary information, changing targets at short notice)
- Belittling someone's opinion
- Making false accusations
- Monitoring work unnecessarily, intrusively or unfairly
- Humiliating someone in front of others
- Ostracism
- Use of 'flame-mail' (bullying via email).

Box 5.20 includes some of the most common forms that workplace bullying can take.

The impact of harassment and bullying

Harassment and bullying damage both individuals and the organizations which employ them. The victims may suffer loss of confidence and self-esteem and become demotivated, leading to a reduction in the quality and quantity of their work. Their health may suffer as a result of unhealthy stress, leading to increased sickness absence. The study conducted by Hoel and Cooper found that those who reported that they had been bullied were significantly more likely to report high levels of mental ill health than those who had not been bullied. Ultimately, those who are harassed or bullied may feel that the only way to stop the unwanted behaviour is to leave the organization. For the organization, harassment and bullying results in increased absenteeism, demoralization, damage to staff relations, increased staff turnover and, if victims seek legal redress, damage to its reputation and potentially severe financial penalties.

How to deal with complaints of harassment or bullying

The majority of HE institutions have policies to address harassment and some of these also cover bullying, or there may be a separate policy on bullying. A few institutions have adopted a more comprehensive 'dignity at work' approach. Managers should be aware of their institution's policy, particularly in relation to the procedure to be followed if a complaint of harassment or bullying is made. Don't dismiss a complaint out of hand – be sympathetic and take it seriously. Contact personnel/HR for advice without delay. It may be that the policy provides for all other steps to be carried out by a designated person (for example, a harassment adviser). In the absence of an institutional policy, Box 5.21 sets out the steps to follow if a complaint of harassment or bullying is made.

Box 5.21 How to deal with complaint of harassment or bullying

- Discuss with the complainant whether the matter can be dealt with informally (by a face-to-face discussion with the alleged harasser/bully, or in writing)
- If an informal approach is not appropriate, or has been tried and failed:
  - inform the alleged harasser/bully of the complaint
  - separate the complainant and the alleged harasser/bully, suspending the subject of the complaint if necessary and if permissible in the context of the disciplinary procedure
  - set a concise timetable for resolution of the complaint
  - investigate the complaint: interview, on a confidential basis, both parties, and any witnesses to the alleged harassment/bullying; look for evidence of the effects of harassment/bullying (for example, increased sickness absence, impaired work performance); check whether similar allegations have been made against the alleged harasser/bully in the past
  - if the complaint is well-founded, initiate disciplinary action in accordance with the relevant disciplinary procedure
  - if there is insufficient evidence to support the complaint, this does not necessarily mean that the complaint was malicious or otherwise ill intentioned, but indicative of difficulties in the relationship between the two parties which they should be encouraged to address – however, if there are grounds to suspect that the complaint was malicious then the matter should be investigated and appropriate action taken

---

Conclusion ∎

This chapter has demonstrated that, by tackling problems early and appropriately, disputes can be resolved before they become intractable, the productivity of poorly performing staff can be improved and stress can be addressed before it seriously damages health. It has also been shown that sickness, disability, mental health problems and drug and alcohol dependence can all be handled in ways that allow a member of staff to continue to make a productive and valuable contribution to the organization. However, there are times when, despite everything, things don't work out. For more information see Chapter 7, which looks at the ending of the employment relationship, and how to handle dismissals fairly.

6

MANAGING WORK-LIFE BALANCE[1]
Catherine Simm

Introduction

You've probably heard of 'work-life balance', but what does it mean? The term originated in the late 1990s and describes a concept that was originally seen as a 'women's issue', concerned with family-friendly policies and flexible working practices. However, work-life balance is a holistic approach that goes further and is for everyone, not just women. It recognizes that individuals at all stages of life perform best when allowed to strike their own balance, fine-tuning work commitments with those of their wider lives. Fundamental to the concept is an acknowledgement that what suits one individual won't necessarily suit another.

The business case and the national context

The theory behind work-life balance suggests that there should be no constraints and no boundaries to flexibility. It is a strategic, deliberate step towards increased competitiveness, achieved through new ways of working. Employers who are serious about work-life balance rely on it to give them a competitive edge in the marketplace. They typically adopt an integrated approach and have a portfolio of policies and working practices under the work-life balance banner in their 'organizational toolkit'. True supporters of work-life balance believe it is a win-win approach, with benefits to both employees and employers alike.

The UK has the longest working hours in Europe.[2] The HSE estimate that stress is now the second biggest cause of work related illness in the UK and that British industry loses £370 million every year to stress related illness. A survey conducted by the Department of Trade and Industry's Work-life Balance Campaign and *Management Today*[3] in 2002 found that:

- given the chance, employees said they would rather work more flexible hours than win the lottery;
- one in five workers wanted a better work-life balance;
- there had been a steep rise in the number of people who work excessive hours over the previous two years;
- seven out of ten workers who described themselves as stressed did not have access to formal flexible working practices.

Research indicates that work-life balance makes good business sense as it leads to an increase in productivity. A report[4] written by the University of Bradford and the UK Centre for Economic and Environmental Development in 2002, based on findings from employees participating in a home working scheme run by British Telecom, revealed that 90 per cent of workers said that their productivity had increased. The reasons given for the productivity gains included reduced disruption, reduced commuting time and greater flexibility about where and when to work. Workers also reported having more leisure time and finding it easier to help around the home. Twenty-two per cent of participating employees reported having worked at home when they had felt too ill to travel to work. Other companies are reporting benefits, too. For example, Northern Rock found that staff turnover rates in one of its call centres were reduced by 27 per cent after the introduction of work-life balance policies.[5]

Work-life balance in HE

Work-life balance has not been a major issue in HE, partly because of the high degree of flexibility and control over working life enjoyed by its core workforce – the academic staff. However, the issues facing the sector are changing and work-life balance is moving up the agenda. Academic staff (and other staff groups) are working increasingly long hours and are proving difficult to recruit and retain. In 1993, the Association of University Teachers (AUT) warned that a 'retirement time-bomb' was 'ticking at the heart of the higher education system'. The younger generation, the so-called Generation X, believe that work is only one element in their total life experience and are increasingly unwilling to sacrifice all other aspects for employment prospects.[6]

The labour markets from which universities and colleges recruit range from local to national and international, depending on the staff group. Recruiting the highest calibre of staff is not easy. To attract the best staff, HEIs have to offer something different. With nationally agreed terms and conditions of employment, differentiation is not easy. Universities, like other public sector employers, have to turn their attention to other factors that will enrich the working lives of their employees. It is now becoming more important to get work-life balance right.

The unique peaks and troughs of the academic year are well-known and some types of flexible working, such as termtime working, casual workers, bank staff (for example, hourly paid teaching staff and invigilators) and the long-standing tradition of academic staff working from home, have been prevalent in the HE sector for many years. Many employers need a flexible workforce to meet customer needs and demands and stay in business, and HEIs are no exception. The demand for different ways of learning such as distance and online, the focus on the 'student experience' and the increasingly competitive environment, have all been key drivers for change in HE. The increased use of and developments in IT have made new ways of learning and teaching possible but have revolutionized the ways in which universities and colleges work. For example, to make online and distance learning possible, backup services such as library and IT facilities are needed to cover extended periods, in some cases 24 hours a day, seven days a week.

This chapter will take a practical look at work-life balance in the HE sector by examining the impact of the relevant legislation, illustrated by fictional case studies and actual case law, and by looking at some of the findings from recent relevant research.

The Flexible Employment Options project

In 1997, the Commission on University Career Opportunity (CUCO), a working group of the Committee of Vice-Chancellors and Principals (now known as Universities UK), published a set of guidelines called *Flexible Working in Universities and Higher Education Colleges*. The group had undertaken a survey and concluded that, although flexible working was a strength, the balance of flexibility had been too much in favour of the employer and contributed to overwork, stress and job insecurity.

In 1999, as part of the Good Management Initiative, the HEFCE invited bids for project funding. The Flexible Employment Options (FEO) project was established as a result of a joint bid between four HEIs: the University of Birmingham, Canterbury Christ Church

University College, De Montfort University and Staffordshire University. The FEO project team's brief was to develop a programme of flexible employment options specifically suited to the HE sector, building on the earlier research carried out by the CUCO.

In March 2001, the FEO project team conducted a survey of flexible employment policies and practices in all HEIs within the UK. Fifty institutions responded to the questionnaire (a response rate of 42 per cent). The data was used to establish a picture of the frequency of particular flexible employment policies and practices within the sector and also to contribute towards the identification of best practice case studies. The results of the survey provided a useful baseline from which universities and colleges could benchmark their own practices for the first time.

The conclusions drawn from the survey results were:

- flexible working practices in HE were widespread, but were largely informal;
- a change in culture would be needed to encourage acceptance of some types of arrangement and to maximize the benefits derived from them;
- differential treatment across staff groups was commonplace (for example, flexitime was typically available only to support staff);
- there were marked differences in practices between the pre- and post-1992 parts of the sector – for example, provision for time off for public duties was commonplace in the new university sector (due to their historical links to local authority control) but rarer in the pre-1992 part of the sector.

The survey revealed that 11 universities appeared to be performing better than the rest in terms of work-life balance. Further research was undertaken at those universities from which five then emerged as 'best practice sites'.[7] Findings from these best practice universities will be discussed in more detail later in the chapter.

Other work-life balance projects in HE

In 2000, the HEFCE set aside an additional £330 million over three years to improve the management of human resources in HE under the Rewarding and Developing Staff in Higher Education initiative. Many universities followed in the FEO project team's footsteps by investing some of this money in work-life balance initiatives. Many other projects in individual universities and colleges have also been supported by Department of Trade and Industry Challenge funds.

The impact of legislation on work-life balance ▮

The UK has seen many changes in employment legislation in recent years. It could be argued that the changes implemented during the late 1990s, and up to the time of writing, tilted the balance of the employment relationship in favour of employees, in line with practice in other European countries. The government of the time wanted to make it easier for parents to work and this was the underlying reason for many of the amendments that were made. If an employee feels they have been unfairly treated they are protected by these laws and are able to make a claim to an employment tribunal[8] as long as they have one year's service with an employer (in most cases).

This section[9] will focus on the recent changes to statutory provisions covering maternity, paternity and adoption leave and then look at some less well-known types of 'family-friendly' leave, namely parental leave, time off to care for dependants and the rights for working parents introduced by the Employment Act 2002. It will also take a brief look at some other key pieces of recent legislation: the Part-time Workers (Prevention of Unfavourable Treatment) Regulations 2000; the Fixed-term Employees (Prevention of Unfavourable Treatment) Regulations 2002; and the Human Rights Act 1998. Lastly, an analysis of key legislation would not be complete without an examination of the SDA 1975, the most influential piece of legislation in this area to date.

Maternity leave and pay

Significant changes to the rules on maternity leave and pay, made in order to make them easier to understand and simpler to administer, came into effect in April 2003 and are summarized in Box 6.1.

An employee must inform her employer of her pregnancy and the date on which she intends to start her leave during the fifteenth week before the expected week of childbirth (EWC) – this is called the Notification Week. This allows the employer to calculate the length of leave and the return date with certainty. However, the employee can adjust the start date of her maternity leave as long as she gives four weeks' notice of her intended start date.

If a woman is off sick for pregnancy related reasons at any time during the four weeks before the EWC, the start of the maternity leave is automatically triggered even if the sickness is one day long.

The qualification requirements for maternity leave and pay are summarized in Table 6.1.

Box 6.1 Key features of the framework for maternity pay and leave from April 2003

- 26 weeks' ordinary leave (paid)
- 26 weeks' additional maternity leave (unpaid)
  = 1 year in total.
- 26 weeks' qualification period for pay and leave
- Notification arrangements harmonized on one date – the fifteenth week before expected week of childbirth (EWC)
- 4 weeks used for all notification periods
- 4 weeks used for sickness trigger (explained above)

Table 6.1 Qualification requirements for statutory maternity leave and pay

Weeks employed by expected week of childbirth (EWC)	Maternity leave	Maternity pay[10]
Less than **41 weeks**	**26 weeks**	If eligible, maternity allowance (MA)
41 weeks or more	**26 weeks** Ordinary maternity leave	If eligible, MA for first 26 weeks
	26 Weeks Additional maternity leave	or
	(Total leave: **1 year**)	If eligible, statutory maternity pay for first **26 weeks** if average weekly earnings in the 8 weeks up to and including the qualifying week have been above the lower earnings limit for National Insurance Contributions

Source: Department of Trade and Industry

'Ordinary leave' is the paid part of maternity leave, 'additional leave' is the unpaid part. Most HEIs have traditionally offered occupational schemes which are superior to the statutory framework and therefore may have been unaffected by these changes. The 2001 FEO survey found that 82 per cent of those institutions that responded offered enhanced maternity provisions. However, it is important to remember that occupational maternity leave and pay provisions vary between staff groups in some HEIs.

It is also important to remember that the contract of employment continues throughout maternity leave unless either party to the contract expressly ends it or it expires. All other terms and conditions of employment apart from remuneration continue. Holiday entitlement accrues while the employee is on maternity leave and individuals may wish to add annual leave onto the end of their maternity leave to delay their return to work without incurring any financial hardship (see pages 151–152 for more information on women returning from maternity leave).

Paternity leave

From April 2003, fathers have been entitled to two weeks' paid paternity leave paid at the same flat rate as statutory maternity pay. The change in legislation encouraged some employers to review their policies and to offer paternity leave on full pay. Of the HE institutions which took part in the 2001 FEO survey, 78 per cent offered some form of paternity leave. Some HEIs have offered paid leave of between three and five days for a number of years, but up until April 2003, two weeks' paid leave was rare.

It is worth noting that new fathers have the option of taking two weeks' paid paternity leave followed by four weeks of unpaid parental leave, following the birth of their child, giving them six weeks in total to spend with their new child and partner. Employers should plan for this and indeed remind new fathers that they have these rights. In cases of adoption, the two weeks' 'paternity' leave can actually be taken by the mother when the father elects to take the longer period of adoption leave. These aspects of the legislation are significant as they recognize the increasing importance of the role that fathers play in the child rearing process in today's society.

Adoption leave

Up until 2001, adoptive parents were not entitled to the full extent of leave or any of the financial support that was available to natural birth parents. However, HEIs have traditionally offered more generous provisions to adoptive parents than those that were available by law. Of those respondents that took part in the 2001 FEO survey, 60 per cent offered some form of adoption leave, but typically these fell short of maternity provisions. The key provisions of statutory adoption leave are set out in Box 6.2.

Box 6.2 Key features of adoption leave

- 26 weeks' adoption leave paid at flat rate statutory maternity pay
- 26 weeks' additional unpaid adoption leave

  = 1 year in total

- 2 weeks' paid leave around the time of placement (equivalent to paternity leave)
- Available to those adopting children up to 18 years of age
- The employee must have worked for the employer for 26 weeks before notification to qualify

---

The provisions of adoption leave and pay now mirror those of maternity provisions. Adoption leave is paid at the same rate as statutory maternity pay, starting when a child is first placed with the family. Adoptive parents are able to choose which of the parents takes the time off and receives the payment.

Adoptive parents are eligible to take the leave if the child is under 18 years of age. For siblings that are simultaneously placed with a family, only one period of adoption leave applies. As adoption leave is not required to satisfy the same health and safety requirements as are needed for maternity leave, adoptive parents can decide who is best placed to take the leave.

Universities and colleges wishing to adopt best practice may go one step further by allowing prospective adoptive parents to take parental leave in blocks of one hour or more in the run up to the placement of a child, enabling them to attend meetings and court proceedings. With an average of only 2000 adoptions per year taking place in the UK this is not likely to be a significant burden to any individual employer.

Parental leave

Parental leave was first introduced on 15 December 1999 to give parents of children born or adopted on or after that date the right to take a period of (unpaid) time off work to look after a child or make arrangements for the child's welfare. Parents can use it to spend more time with children and strike a better balance between their work and family commitments. The key features of parental leave are set out in Box 6.3.

Employers have discretion to make their own arrangements as to

---

Box 6.3 Key features of parental leave

- May be taken by parents with a child born on or after 15 December 1999
- One-year qualifying period
- Applies to those with formal parental responsibility
- 13 weeks' parental leave for each child
- Leave may be taken up to the child's fifth birthday (eighteenth for a disabled child) or five years after an adoptive child is placed

---

Box 6.4 The 'fallback scheme' for parental leave

- Leave can be taken in blocks or multiples of one week; parents with a disabled child can take leave one day at a time
- After giving 21 days' notice
- Up to a maximum of four weeks' leave in a year
- May be subject to a postponement by an employer for up to six months for business reasons
- Cannot be postponed when the employee wishes to take it immediately after the time the child is born or placed for adoption

---

how this leave may be taken in practice. In the HE sector it is likely that such arrangements will usually be agreed with the recognized trade unions. Agreements may improve the key elements set out above but cannot offer less. Where such an agreement does not exist the 'fallback scheme', outlined in Box 6.4, must be used.

The key feature of parental leave is that, unlike time off to care for dependants (see the next section), it is *planned*.

Time off to care for dependants (Employment Relations Act 1999)

The right to time off to care for dependants, which allows employees to take a reasonable amount of time off work to deal with certain unexpected or sudden emergencies and to make any longer-term arrangements which may be needed, is contained in Section 57A of the Employment Rights Act 1996, as amended by the Employment Relations Act 1999. The emergency must involve a dependant of the employee. There is no limit to the amount of time off someone can have, as it is intended to cover genuine emergencies. Unlike other entitlements (such as parental leave) employees do not have to meet any qualification requirements to take time off to care for dependants. All employees have this right from day one of their employment.

The circumstances in which leave may be taken are outlined in Box 6.5.

Like parental leave, the time off is unpaid – employers may choose to pay for it if they wish, but this is relatively uncommon in HE. Only 28 per cent of respondents who took part in the 2001 FEO survey offered additional benefits on top of the statutory ones. Some organizations, however, have traditionally offered special or compassionate leave (for example, in times of bereavement or when caring for a terminally ill relative). While such leave is often paid, it usually requires the approval of the head of department.

Although both parental leave and time off to care for dependants are unpaid, it is a recognition that employees often need to be away from the workplace for reasons other than sickness and that this is sometimes out of their control. Statistics indicate that time off to care for dependants and parental leave are rarely taken up, because they are unpaid. However, the value of both these types of leave should not be underestimated and employees should be offered parental or dependant leave in appropriate circumstances. It avoids employees from having to use annual leave for things such as child care emergencies, or from taking sick leave, which may not reflect well on either their sickness record or the organization's sickness absence figures. The case study in Box 6.6 gives an example of a situation where leave to care for dependants may be useful.

Box 6.5 The circumstances in which time off to care for dependants may be taken

- If a dependant falls ill, or has been injured or assaulted
- When a dependant is having a baby
- To make longer-term arrangements for a dependant who is ill or injured
- To deal with the death of a dependant
- To deal with an unexpected disruption or breakdown of care arrangements for a dependant
- To deal with an unexpected incident involving the employee's child during school hours

---

Box 6.6   Case study 1 – time off to care for dependants

Dr W is a senior lecturer who normally leaves home after his child-minder arrives to look after his two young children. One morning, his childminder called to say that she had had a car accident and was unable to work for the rest of the week. Dr W needed to stay with his children until he could find someone to look after them. He phoned the departmental secretary to tell her that he had been delayed and he would come into work as soon as he was able. Dr W returned to work that afternoon once alternative arrangements for child care had been put in place and told his head of department that he had made arrangements for his mother-in-law to come to stay with him for the week to look after the children. However, he needed to collect her from the train station the following morning and therefore he would not be able to come into work until later on. In total, he was absent for six and a half hours to deal with this emergency.

Legally, Dr W was entitled to the time off to deal with this emergency, as it clearly falls within the remit of time off to care for dependants. The question for the employer is whether or not the leave should be paid. This will depend upon the organization's policy on time off to care for dependants, which should state whether the time should be paid or unpaid. In the absence of such a policy a common-sense approach is advocated. If the head of department is able to exercise discretion then it would seem sensible not to require Dr W to take these few missed hours as unpaid dependant leave. It would almost certainly result in an administrative burden that would outweigh any cost savings, and it is likely that the time lost will be recouped at a later date.

The Employment Act 2002 – Rights for working parents

This piece of legislation pulls together several key themes that have underpinned much of the legislation that preceded it. The Labour government wanted employers to cooperate with its drive for flexibility rather than forcing them to do so through legislation. The Employment Act 2002 stopped short of giving working parents the *right* to work flexibly but it gave them the right to *request* to do so.

From April 2003, parents with children under the age of 6 have had the right to request a variation in their contract so that they can work

---

Box 6.7   The right to request flexible working

Applies to any employee who:
- has 26 weeks' continuous service at the date of application
- has a child who is under 6 (18 if disabled)
- is responsible for the upbringing of the child
- is the biological parent, guardian, adopter or foster carer of the child or is married to, or the partner of, one of the above and living with the child

---

more flexibly in relation to their hours, times and place of work. In practice, this means that employers have a duty to consider requests seriously and are able to refuse only where there is a clear, justifiable business reason. If a change is agreed it will be permanent and there will be no right to revert back to the former arrangement. If a request is rejected a further request cannot be made for 12 months. Qualification rights are laid down in Box 6.7.

A request to work flexibly under the new regulations will be made under Section 80F of the Employment Rights Act 1996. The onus is on the individual to set out the working pattern that they wish to adopt and explain the effect that they envisage it will have on their employer and how they may accommodate it. If the employer refuses the request, a full explanation must be given. The case study in Box 6.8 sets out an example of a request to work flexibly.

A key consideration for employers will be whether to restrict this right to those employees with children under the age of 6 as laid down in the regulations, or whether to extend the right to all working parents, or to all employees regardless of whether they have children or not. Those employers who are truly in favour of work-life balance would argue that there is no justification for restricting this right to employees with children under 6, as the bottom line is that if any employee feels there are adjustments that can be made to their working pattern to help their work-life balance then these adjustments should also benefit the organization.

SDA 1975

Those employees who do not have children under the age of 6 who request a change to their working hours/patterns which is rejected may rely upon the SDA 1975 to make a claim of unfair treatment. With the plethora of new legislation introduced in recent years it

---

Box 6.8   Case study 2 – the right to request flexible working

---

Ms A is a catering manager at a large university which has three campuses all within close proximity of each other. Her office is based at the main campus in the city centre, and she leaves home early in the morning to get to work for 9 a.m. On a typical day Ms A makes at least one trip to another campus, taking at least 30 minutes travelling time and then travels back to her office for the rest of the day. On the way home she collects her daughter from nursery and returns home after 6 p.m. most evenings. Ms A is often tired as her days are long and involve quite a lot of travelling. She feels that her work-life balance could easily be improved by making a few minor adjustments to her working arrangements. She has asked her line manager about this previously but has always had her suggestions refused as he was concerned about 'setting a precedent'.

Ms A makes a request under Section 80F of the Employment Rights Act 1996 to vary her place of work. She sets out the impact that she thinks it will have on her employer. She asks if she can work from home on occasions and sets out an example of a typical day. She would come into the office in the morning as normal, and travel to the second campus as usual, but then instead of returning to her office she would travel home and work from there for the remainder of the day. She can check her emails on her own computer, she has already been provided with a mobile phone to allow her staff to contact her and she would be able to work on reports and reviews without constant interruptions. This would give her more quality time with her daughter in the evening, and allow her to catch up with paperwork later on as she would not feel as tired. Ms A notes in her application that this would free up her office to be used for other purposes. She explains that on a typical day these new arrangements would create an extra hour and a half's productive time, and would therefore be of great benefit both to herself and to her employer.

As the request has been made formally under Section 80F, her line manager is obliged to give it full consideration, and the argument that it would 'set a precedent' is not a justifiable reason to refuse it (see the example in Box 6.12). It would be very difficult for Ms A's line manager to turn down this request, as there are clearly benefits to both parties.

Box 6.9 *Marshall v. Devon County Council* [2000][11]

Mrs Marshall worked as a headteacher at a primary school and wished to return to work on a job-share basis after her maternity leave. The school governors considered the request but rejected it on the grounds that a recent Office for Standards in Education (Ofsted) report had identified the school as one with serious weaknesses and they felt that one person, not two, should be in overall charge. The employment tribunal ruled in favour of Mrs Marshall stating that refusing her to allow to return to work on a job-share basis was sex discrimination.

---

would be easy to forget the pioneering discrimination laws introduced in the 1970s. However, it is these tried and tested laws which in reality continue to offer employees the best protection against unfair treatment. See the example from case law in Box 6.9.

The main basis of the SDA is that it is unlawful to discriminate on the grounds of sex or marital status. The key for most successful claims has been the ability of women to claim indirect discrimination rather than direct discrimination. Indirect discrimination occurs when a condition or requirement is imposed, even unintentionally, which cannot be objectively justified, with which a considerably smaller proportion of women (or men) can comply, and which results in a detriment to the person who cannot comply with it.

Employers are particularly vulnerable to claims of sex discrimination when dealing with requests for part-time working and for requests to work from home (see *Marshall v. Devon County Council*, above, and *Lockwood v. Crawley Warren Group Ltd*, (see page 153). This is because the requirement to work full-time is a condition with which fewer women than men can comply and is to the woman's detriment because her child care responsibilities prevent her from complying with it.

The only way that an employer can defend a claim of sex discrimination is by arguing that there was an objective business reason for turning down the request or insisting that a job has to be done full-time or at a certain place of work. Many of the traditional arguments that once would have succeeded at employment tribunal are becoming increasingly difficult to sustain. For example, to argue that a job is too senior for a job-share no longer holds water (see *Marshall v. Devon County Council*). An analysis of recent employment tribunal decisions of cases about access to variations to hours of work (such as requests for changes to working patterns to meet child care needs) reveals high success rates (56 per cent in 1999 and 44 per cent in 2000).

Human Rights Act 1998

Employees can also make claims of unfair treatment with respect to child care arrangements under the Human Rights Act (HRA). The HRA became law in October 2000 and covers a wide range of issues. Article 8, the right to respect for private and family life, is the most relevant part of the act in terms of working arrangements. Again, if a require-ment is imposed on an employee (such as working full time) an indi-vidual can argue they are being deprived of the right to a private life. As this law only came in force in 2000 it is yet to be fully tested in the courts and tribunals, but should be taken into consideration during the decision making process.

Part-time Workers (Prevention of Less Favourable Treatment) Regulations 2000

These regulations came into force in 2000. The aim, as the title sug-gests, is to remove any discrimination against part-time workers. The regulations cover such aspects of employment as overtime pay, sick pay, maternity pay, holiday pay, access to pension schemes, training opportunities, career break schemes and selection criteria for redun-dancy. Employers need to ensure that they are not treating part-time workers less favourably than their full-time colleagues. One example would be if a training course was scheduled to last for two full days preventing a part-time worker who was only able to work for part of the day from attending. This is because it could be said to be denying that individual a training opportunity which may later hinder their career progression. This piece of legislation is significant as it gave positive rights to part-time employees for the first time.

Work-life balance in practice ▐

Dealing with requests

A useful starting point for employers is to think about how they can accommodate a request to work flexibly, rather than how they can turn it down. This is the approach advocated by Leeds Metropolitan University and goes some way to explaining why they won the regional Parents at Work award in 2001 for being a 'family-friendly' employer. This premise is endorsed by Oxford Brookes University who 'always try to say yes to a request' and Middlesex University who say they have 'a genuine desire to find out what employees actually want'. All three universities were identified as 'best practice sites' by the FEO project. Although each request from an employee is unique, there are always a number of key things to bear in mind when considering a request, and a number of pitfalls to avoid.

Considerations to bear in mind

The university or college's personnel and HR policies should support and guide managers and departmental heads through the decision making process and the implications. They should clearly state what the policy of the university or college is on a particular issue, and which elements are left to the line manager's discretion. The first step, therefore, is to consult the organization's personnel procedures or contact the personnel department for guidance.

Managers and heads of department need to follow a consistent approach when considering requests from employees so that they can demonstrate that everyone has had an equal opportunity to apply for flexible working arrangements and that a clear and fair process has been followed. It is important that the decision making process is documented in case of possible challenges at a later stage in the process. A manager's checklist is suggested in Box 6.10.

Box 6.10 A manager's checklist when considering requests for flexible working

---

- Is there a clear policy on this type of flexible working?
- How will the work/post, needs of the business/service be covered?
- What impact will the request have on others in the team?
- What are the implications for communication within the team?
- Is this employee skilled enough to make this work?
- Is this post particularly suited to flexible working?
- What arrangements do other members of the team have at present?
- Is it a reasonable request? Are there more reasons to say 'yes' than to say 'no', that is, do the benefits outweigh the drawbacks?

The Employment Act 2002 puts the onus on individuals making requests to prove that it will work for both parties. Employees are obliged to explain in their application the effect they envisage it will have on the employer. Employees requesting flexible working arrangements should, therefore, also be encouraged to work through and answer some of the questions on this checklist. Once the employee has thought it through from the employer's point of view they should be able to identify any potential pitfalls and ensure that their request is reasonable and practical. It is in their interests to do so as once they have made an application they have no right to submit another for 12 months.

Clear and detailed feedback as to why a particular request has been refused should enable the employee to understand and accept the reasons and reduce the scope for conflict. In fact, research conducted by the FEO team found little resentment from staff that were not able to work flexibly as long as schemes and methods of application were perceived to be fair.

Trial periods

In years gone by it was usually only employers who came up with new ways of working, sometimes trying to impose them on a reluctant workforce. Nowadays employees have equal rights to suggest new ways of working and this can be difficult for some managers to come to terms with. It is not uncommon for managers to be sceptical when new ways of working are suggested to them, just as employees can be sceptical when they are asked to vary their working hours and patterns.

After working through the checklist above, if there is still some doubt as to whether a new way of working will be successful, the best way to find out is to try it. A four-week trial period should be sufficient in most cases to give an indication as to whether or not a particular scheme or work pattern will be successful. There are clearly benefits to both sides in having a trial period. The employee can see if it suits them and the manager can assess the impact on the work. The criteria that will be used to judge success or failure should be clearly laid down at the beginning of the trial period and regular reviews should take place throughout. If the trial period is judged not to have been a success, a manager will have concrete reasons for refusing the request which will be more readily accepted, as the employee will feel that they were given a fair chance.

Pitfalls to avoid – the most common fears

Setting a precedent

The most common fear of a manager is that of 'setting a precedent', that is, if they say yes to one request to adopt a particular working pattern from an individual they will have to say yes to all others. In work-life balance there should be no such thing as setting a precedent, as each individual case should be judged on its own merits (see the example from case law, *Wright* v. *Rugby Borough Council*, in Box 6.12). Once one individual's request to work flexibly is agreed, the dynamics and working practices of that particular team or department will change accordingly, so it may not be possible to agree the next request that is made.

Challenges for the manager

It is important that managers are honest with themselves when dealing with a request. If the real reason that a manager is reluctant to approve a request is because it will make their own life more difficult and they would rather maintain the *status quo*, this needs to be acknowledged. Then, and only then, will it become apparent that the *status quo* may no longer be an option, as refusing a request may result in a demotivated, dissatisfied employee. Flexible working inevitably entails more complicated managerial processes in terms of communication, control, coordination and planning, so managers can be forgiven for being apprehensive. However, it is important to remember that the opposite of flexibility is *in*flexibility. Refusing a request made by an employee who feels that their work-life balance needs are not being met may mean that they look to another employer who may better meet their needs.[12]

Fear of abuse

Many managers are reluctant to move away from working patterns which allow for close supervision and monitoring towards patterns that allow for greater freedoms along with flexibility. Any policy or procedure can be abused, whether it is the flexitime scheme, occupational sick pay or business expenses procedure. Contrary to popular belief, flexible working practices are no more prone to abuse than any other areas of employment. However, it will be harder to spot an employee who leaves work before completing their contracted hours when there are staggered start and finish times, than if all employees leave at 5 p.m. when the office closes. It is up to the manager to keep a tight control on this as with all aspects of employee conduct. Managers must ensure that they manage flexible work arrangements and that flexible work arrangements don't manage them. For example, the rules of the scheme can be drawn up so that, during predicted workload peaks, accrued flexitime is carried forward, rather than being taken at a time when it would cause operational difficulty. Similarly, the scheme should be designed in such a way that employees are not able to 'bank' flexitime when there is insufficient work to warrant the extra hours. Managers must make it clear to employees that proven abuse of flexible working practices is taken seriously and considered to be misconduct liable to lead to disciplinary action.

Flexible working options ∎

There are many different flexible working options, some of which are common in other sectors of the economy but which are relatively new to HE. It is not the intention to give a definitive list here, or to expand on every available option. The aim is to explore the challenges that some of the options pose for operational managers when dealing with requests from employees for flexible working or when trying to implement new ways of working to create a flexible workforce. Some of the most common flexible working options are listed in Box 6.11 and the first five are discussed in more detail.

Flexitime

Flexitime is a well-established and very popular flexible working option. Not surprisingly, it is more common in the post–1992 universities than in the pre-1992 universities, as its initial roots were in the public sector. The 2001 FEO survey revealed that only 38 per cent

---

Box 6.11 Common flexible working options

- Flexitime
- Compressed hours
- Voluntary reduced time
- Working *from* home/*at* home
- Job-share
- Career breaks
- Annualized hours

of respondents had a formal flexitime policy. The survey also revealed that where it does exist, flexitime tends to be restricted to support staff groups.

Flexitime was initially introduced to enable employees to stagger their start and finish times and offer the additional benefit of being able to take shorter or longer lunch breaks and half or full days off work, if enough flexitime has been built up. Each individual flexitime scheme differs according to 'band width' (that is, the earliest start and the latest finish times) and core hours (the minimum times that an employee needs to be present at work).

The main benefit to employees is that they have a much better opportunity to manage their work and personal commitments and interests than if they work fixed hours. This is the whole premise behind work-life balance and therefore flexitime is a good starting point. It fosters team cooperation as colleagues tend to make arrangements between themselves to ensure minimum staffing levels are maintained while accommodating their leave requirements. For employers, it minimizes time lost through employees attending routine medical appointments and through minor disruptions to child care or travel arrangements. It also puts the onus on individuals to manage their own time, with intervention only necessary when problems arise.

The example from case law in Box 6.12 demonstrates that a flexitime scheme should be simply that – flexible.

Compressed working hours

Compressed working hours is where a full-time post is condensed into less than five days a week. Typically an employee will work a nine-day

---

Box 6.12 *Wright v. Rugby Borough Council* [1984][13]

Ms Wright's normal hours were 8.45 a.m. to 5.15 p.m. with one hour for lunch. Following her return from maternity leave she asked to work from 8.30 a.m. to 4.30 p.m. with only half an hour for lunch. The council granted this on a temporary basis but refused to make it a permanent arrangement as they said it would affect their flexitime policy and set an undesirable precedent. The tribunal found that the flexitime scheme was irrelevant and saw no reason why it should set an undesirable precedent and therefore decided that Ms Wright had been discriminated against under the SDA.

Box 6.13   Case study 3 – compressed working week

Mrs B is a faculty manager. She works long hours, building up time in lieu that she is rarely able to take. She arrives at work early and leaves late, partly through choice, as she commutes and so avoids the traffic, but partly because of the demands of the job. She often attends examination boards and committee meetings which run on after office hours. Mrs B has recently suffered some ill health and the dean of faculty feels she may well be at risk of burn-out. The dean suggests that Mrs B works a nine-day fortnight, whereby she works just over eight and a quarter hours a day for nine rather than ten days. This means that she benefits from having a long weekend every other week and a chance to recover from the pressures of work. This is a healthy, but realistic, option for the faculty, as it recognizes that it is often difficult for Mrs B to get away on time but attempts to address the problem of the long hours she puts in. It is also likely to reduce her stress levels, make her more effective while she is at work and encourage a healthier lifestyle, thus avoiding sickness absence problems in the future.

---

fortnight rather than a ten-day fortnight. They continue to receive a full-time salary and the only implications are for the calculation of annual leave (better calculated as hours rather than full days) and for health and safety, such as ensuring adequate rest breaks. The benefits of compressed working hours to employees are less travelling time to and from work and longer rest breaks at the weekend. The benefits to the employer are not as obvious but include a reduction in stress levels, avoiding possible burn-out and a positive move away from a long hours culture. The case study in Box 6.13 demonstrates this. Compressed working in support functions may also allow extended service hours on some days of the week.

Voluntary reduced time

Employees will often request a change to their working hours/ patterns when their personal circumstances change and they are no longer able to work full-time – for example, women returning from maternity leave. A number of options are available to ease women returners back into the workplace and avoid their skills being lost altogether. After maternity leave an employee may wish to take a further four weeks unpaid parental leave and/or period of annual leave prior to returning. Some employees may wish to delay their return further by taking a career break, or if this is not possible, they may wish to return on a permanent part-time basis. However, they may wish to reduce their hours for a temporary period only, while their child is young. They could use their annual leave entitlement to enable them to work part-time for a short period of time. Alternatively, if they wish to reduce their hours temporarily, but on a longer term basis, this is known as voluntary reduced time, or 'v-time'. This flexible working option is very common as relatively few women want to give up work altogether after having a baby, but find it difficult to balance full-time work and family responsibilities.

Working *from* home/*at* home

Working from home is the most radical of flexible working options as, unlike other options which simply vary the hours of work, this option, as the name suggests, varies the place of work. In the HE sector it is a benefit traditionally reserved for academics and senior managers, yet it could easily be extended to other staff groups. However, working from home changes fundamentally the way in which an employee is managed. It requires a great deal of trust, excellent organizational and communication skills, and a skilful, enlightened manager who manages by objectives and outputs rather than by supervision. It can be an excellent way of improving productivity for those who undertake project work or report writing which is considerably easier in a peaceful environment, free from interruptions. Likewise, it can minimize time lost for those who spend time travelling between different locations.

The extent of home working can vary between occasional working at home once a month or once a week (known as working *from* home), to working *at* home on a permanent basis and relinquishing office space at work. Working from home/at home requires a great deal of investment in IT to be successful. There are also health and safety implications (particularly in respect of the safe use of computer equipment) as the employer is still responsible for the employee's safety while working at home. The example in Box 6.14 gives a clear reminder that an employer who refuses a request to vary the place of work could fall foul of the law.

Box 6.14   *Lockwood v. Crawley Warren Group Ltd* [2000][14]

Mrs L had to give up full-time work when her mother was no longer able to look after her young baby. Mrs L's offer to work at home (buying her own equipment) or to take six months' unpaid leave was met with a counter-offer of two weeks' leave in order to make alternative child care arrangements. The EAT ruled that the law on indirect sex discrimination put a burden on the employer to justify refusing to allow an application for reduced hours or working from home where this is for child care reasons. In other words, a request to work from home is analogous to a request to work part-time and the burden of proof is on the employer to justify turning down such a request.

Job-share

A job-share arrangement is when two or more people undertake the full range of accountabilities and responsibilities involved in one specific job. Job sharing is an ideal solution where a job needs the cohesion and consistency of full-time cover, but one full-time employee is not available to provide it. Evidence reveals that it can work at any level in an organization, even at director (or equivalent) level. Yet, of all flexible working options, this one is reported to be least favoured by managers. Like working from home, it requires a skilled manager to get the most out of a job-share arrangement – to ensure that effective communication strategies are employed and that handovers are managed well. Equally, both partners in the job-share need to be skilled to make the arrangement work. Also, adequate resourcing of the handover does entail an additional cost, whether this is in terms of an overlap period when both job-sharers are present, or in time spent writing handover notes by one job-sharer for the other. The benefits of the arrangement to the organization, however, include cover for annual leave (and possibly sickness), a wider knowledge base for the job-shared role and synergies arising from two minds and skill sets brought to bear upon the job. In short, the whole package often does amount to more than the sum of its parts.

The benefits and drawbacks of flexible working ▪

The benefits and drawbacks of work-life balance both for employees and employers have been discussed throughout this chapter. It is fair to say that the benefits of flexible working for both employees and employers far outweigh the drawbacks – however, this is not to say that there are none and it is important to acknowledge them.

Benefits to employees

Each specific flexible working option brings with it its own benefits. For example, termtime working allows employees a long break over the summer and removes the problem of child care during school holidays; flexitime allows employees the opportunity to vary their working arrangements on a daily basis and to pursue leisure activities in their free time. However, collectively the benefits of flexible working can be grouped together under a number of key headings. These are summarized in Box 6.15.

Drawbacks for employees

Each particular flexible working scheme brings with it drawbacks. For example, there is the possibility that in order to retain the 'benefit' of working from home an employee will feel that they have to put in excessively long hours; with home working comes the potential for isolation and loneliness and the blurred distinction between home and work life, making it difficult to 'switch off'; with increased flexibility from the employer comes increasing demands for flexibility from the employee – in the days of 24 hours a days seven day a week working there will always be unsociable hours that do not suit any individual but will need to be covered; others in the organization who are not participating in a form of flexible working may have negative perceptions of those that are, believing that they have received preferential treatment, which can result in conflict within teams. Research also shows that many worry that opting for work-life

---

Box 6.15 Benefits of flexible working to employees

- Improved health
- Job satisfaction
- Less stress arising from problems with care arrangements
- Ability to pursue outside interests and have an enriched life
- Improved morale from increased trust

Box 6.16   Possible drawbacks of flexible working for employees

- Potential for exploitation by the employer
- Increasing demands for flexibility
- Isolation
- Blurred distinction between work and home life
- Hostility and resentment from others
- Perceived damage to career prospects

balance damages career prospects.[15] The main drawbacks of flexible working are summarized in Box 6.16.

Benefits to employers

Respondents to the FEO survey gave a variety of reasons for introducing flexible working arrangements. These centred around two main themes: recruitment and retention and meeting customer/service needs. Those identified as best practice sites (and it is worth noting that all are found in the post-1992 part of the sector) identified a desire to be seen as an employer of choice and noted difficulties in attracting staff due to competition from other major local employers. They said that nationally-determined pay and conditions meant that they had little in the way of financial incentives, but what they could offer in terms of flexible working far exceeded that of competitors. A summary of benefits to universities and colleges is outlined in Box 6.17, all of which were cited by one or more of the best practice sites.

Drawbacks for employers

The FEO survey also revealed some drawbacks for employers. The examples given in Box 6.18 were all cited by the best practice sites.

Conclusion ∎

There is no doubt that work-life balance is moving up the agenda in HE, as in all other sectors of the economy. Legislation introduced in recent years cannot be ignored and there is also a sound business case for work-life balance. Flexibility is already very much part of the culture in HE, but only some staff currently benefit from it. Because it

---

Box 6.17 Some benefits of flexible working for employers

- Work-life balance gives a competitive edge leading to improved recruitment (resulting in a reputation as an employer of choice)
- Increased employee commitment and loyalty (possibly arising from increased job satisfaction)
- Increase in productivity, goodwill and flexibility (employees put increased time and effort into their work, as they don't want to lose the flexibility they have gained)
- Reduced costs (arising from: reduced sickness absence, reduced overtime costs as enhanced pay rates are not paid for flexitime, lower turnover rates leading to lower recruitment and training costs)
- Reduced stress levels
- Reduction in need for office space
- Contributes to the equal opportunities/diversity agenda
- Aids compliance with legislation, avoiding costly employment tribunal claims

---

Box 6.18 Potential drawbacks of flexible working for employers

- Needs experienced, skilled managers to manage by objectives rather than supervision
- Needs complete culture change and commitment from the top – cannot be changed overnight
- Employee relations can be damaged if requests aren't dealt with competently or a consistent approach is not followed
- More problematic to arrange meetings etc.
- Communications require extra effort
- Additional costs from set up of schemes and teething troubles
- Schemes can be hijacked or manipulated by employees

---

exists, largely, in piecemeal form and operates on an informal basis, it is difficult to ensure consistency of treatment within the organization and for the potential benefits to both employee and employer to be fully realized. A holistic approach, and integration with institutional objectives, is needed if flexible working practices leading to improved work-life balance are to succeed and for real gains to be made. Many lessons can be learned from those in the HE sector who have adopted such an approach.

As stated in the introduction to this chapter, work-life balance recognizes that individuals perform best when allowed to strike their own balance between work and other aspects of their lives. For more information on the role of management in getting the best out of the biggest asset of any university or college – its staff – see Chapter 4. Chapter 5 addresses some of the problems that can arise from work-life *imbalance,* such as stress and drug or alcohol abuse.

Further information on the FEO project can be found on www.staffs.ac.uk/feo.

MANAGING THE TERMINATION OF EMPLOYMENT

Introduction

All employment relationships come to an end. This might be after a significant period of time, through retirement at normal retirement age, or sooner, by resignation, mutual agreement or, less frequently, by dismissal. In the majority of cases, the parting of the ways between an employer and employee is entirely straightforward (although it is surprising how often the personnel or HR department is not informed that someone has left, the head of department in which they worked presumably believing that telepathy will ensure that they are taken off the payroll at the appropriate time). However, the ending of some employment relationships is more complicated. Even when they are working closely with their personnel/HR colleagues, line managers in universities and colleges often lack confidence when handling these more complex cases, because they come across them so rarely. One of the purposes of this chapter is to help managers in dealing with these cases, by highlighting the pitfalls which have the potential to turn a complicated dismissal into a messy one. The aim is to ensure that all terminations of employment are fair, even if they can't always be amicable.

In this chapter, the ending of the employment relationship is put into legal context, including a brief review of academic freedom, tenure and the Model Statute provisions in chartered universities. Advice is given on how to manage a dismissal fairly and consideration is also given to the handling of resignations and the potential benefit of exit interviews. Finally, the issue of employment references is addressed.

The legal context ▪

An employee is dismissed when the employer terminates the contract of employment. The expiry and non-renewal of a fixed-term contract is also a dismissal and the law applying to the ending of fixed-term contracts is considered below. In some circumstances, the termination of employment by the employee's resignation may be judged to be a dismissal ('constructive dismissal') and this is also considered in more detail below.

Unfair dismissal

It has been said that the introduction of the concept of unfair dismissal in 1971 was the 'most important innovation in employment law' up to that time.[1] Employees with at least one year's continuous service have the right to claim unfair dismissal[2] and a claim must be submitted to an employment tribunal within three months of the effective date of the dismissal. There are three possible remedies if a dismissal is found to be unfair:

- reinstatement (that is, re-employment in the same job and on the same terms and conditions, as if the dismissal had not occurred);
- re-engagement (that is, re-employment in a different job, on terms and conditions that are not necessarily the same as before the dismissal);
- compensation.

Orders for reinstatement or re-engagement normally include an award in respect of compensation for loss of earnings. Compensation awards may be significant, as the statutory limit is in excess of £50,000.

Section 98 of the Employment Rights Act 1996 requires an employer to demonstrate that a dismissal is for one of the following reasons:

- Capability or qualifications of the employee for performing work of the kind which they were employed to do. For example, the dismissal of someone employed as a driver and required to hold a valid driving licence who subsequently had their licence revoked could be justified on this ground.
- Conduct of the employee. For example, the dismissal of someone who had defrauded their employer could be justified on this ground.

- Redundancy. For example, the dismissal of someone undertaking work in which the employer was no longer engaged could be justified on this ground, as can the non-renewal of an externally funded fixed-term contract when the funding has ceased. However, whether the dismissal would be judged to be fair would be subject to other considerations which are discussed further below.
- The employee could not continue to work in the position which they held without contravention (either on their part or on that of the employer) of a duty or restriction imposed by or under an enactment. For example, the dismissal of an overseas national whose right to remain in the UK had expired could be justified on this ground.
- Some other substantial reason (SOSR). For example, a dismissal arising from an irrevocable breakdown in relationships due to a clash of personalities, which was damaging the institution, may be justified on this ground.

If the dismissal is based on more than one ground, the principal reason should be clearly identified. Failure to do so, or to be consistent, may result in the dismissal being found to be unfair. A dismissal that would otherwise have been found to be fair can be found to be unfair if the employer is judged not to have acted reasonably in all circumstances, or to have failed to follow proper procedures, as illustrated by the examples in Box 7.1.

In the example in Box 7.2, action that might, at first glance, appear to be disproportionately harsh, given the nature of the offence, was found to be fair in the light of all the circumstances.

Constructive dismissal

Section 95 (1) of the Employment Relations Act 1999 addresses the concept of constructive dismissal. In this instance, the law regards certain actions of an employer, which amount to a fundamental breach of the contract of employment, as tantamount to a dismissal. Behaviour of this kind entitles the employee to resign and claim unfair dismissal. Examples of conduct that would constitute a fundamental breach of contract include arbitrary demotion, undermining a manager's authority, failure to address a serious grievance, failure to provide a safe system of work and covert monitoring of an employee's telephone calls and/or emails. In order to demonstrate constructive dismissal, the claimant must show that their resignation was as a result of the employer's conduct and that they had not, by continuing to work for the employer for an extended period after the

---

Box 7.1   Unfair dismissal – some examples

Example 1[3]

Mr A was suspended following allegations of indecent exposure. The allegations eventually resulted in a criminal charge against him and he was dismissed without a further meeting with the employer. The EAT held that the employer should have given him another opportunity to explain his conduct before dismissing him.

Example 2[4]

Mr P was a house companion for people with learning difficulties. He was reported by a colleague to have slapped the hand of one of his clients in a local shop. Mr P denied slapping the client; the colleague insisted that he had done so. A witness statement was then submitted which stated that the client was not slapped in the shop. Both Mr P and his colleague were interviewed again and reaffirmed their previous statements, but the witness was not called to give evidence at any point during the investigation. Mr P was dismissed and claimed unfair dismissal. The employment tribunal found that the employers had not conducted a proper investigation.

Example 3[5]

Three employees were dismissed for being involved in a violent argument that had taken place while they were taking part in a two-day seminar. The Court of Appeal found that the employer had overreacted as the misconduct took place out of working hours at the end of an evening of heavy drinking paid for by the company.

Box 7.2   An example of a fair dismissal[6]

Mr O-K worked as a night petrol attendant. Security camera footage showed him taking a damaged packet of cigarettes from a box which was to be returned to the supplier. He was disciplined and dismissed. Although the value of the goods stolen was small, the EAT concluded that the dismissal was within the band of reasonable responses, given that (i) he had been disciplined previously and received warnings, (ii) there were no mitigating circumstances and (iii) he had lied during the disciplinary process.

breach occurred, agreed to it. Box 7.3 includes examples where tribunals have found that the employer's conduct amounted to constructive dismissal.

Fixed-term contracts[7]

The HE sector as a whole has made extensive use of fixed-term contracts over the last two to three decades. In 2001, 30,000–40,000 such staff were employed by HEIs to carry out research,[8] in addition to

---

Box 7.3   Constructive dismissal – examples

Example 1[9]

Ms M, a bakery manager was reprimanded by her manager in front of her staff and customers for not having promotional bread available for sale. She resigned and claimed constructive dismissal. It was found that there had been a breach of the implied term of trust and confidence.

Example 2[10]

Ms R had been bullied and harassed by her manager. As a result of her complaint he was disciplined and required to undergo retraining. The company advised Ms R that he would be moved. However, she met with the company in August 1997 (when she was on sick leave) to discuss her return to work and it became clear that the manager was not going to be moved. She remained on sick leave. There was a further meeting in June 1998 when Ms R realized that the company still had no intention of moving the manager. Two letters from the company followed this meeting which Ms R received in July. One offered her an alternative job, the second advised her that the job was no longer available. Towards the end of July, Ms R resigned and claimed constructive dismissal. The original tribunal found that the company's refusal to move the manager in June 1997 was a serious enough breach of the implied term of trust and confidence to justify Ms R's resignation and claim of constructive dismissal but, by waiting a year before submitting her resignation, she had forfeited that right. The EAT found in Ms R's favour because the refusal to move the manager was just the first in a series of acts that eventually led to a complete breakdown in the relationship between Ms R and the company. The 'final straw' was the second of the two letters that the company sent to her in July 1998.

> **Example 3**[11]
>
> Ms B was engaged to teach Latin. She was told on 27 May that she would be required to teach some French in the forthcoming academic year. Ms B's contract required her to resign by 31 May otherwise she would have to work at least part of the next academic year. She therefore resigned on 28 May and claimed constructive dismissal. The EAT found that requiring Ms B to teach some French was a material change to her job description which should have been the subject of proper consultation with her. In notifying her of the change so close to 31 May, the school had failed to ensure that proper consultation could be carried out by the date on which Ms B had to make her decision regarding her future with the school, and she was constructively dismissed.

smaller numbers of academics and support staff. For much of that time, many of the staff employed on a fixed-term basis were required to waive their rights to a redundancy payment and to claim unfair dismissal, if their fixed-term contract expired and was not renewed. However, the unfair dismissal waiver was abolished by the Employment Relations Act 1999 and the redundancy waiver by the Fixed-term Employees (Prevention of Unfavourable Treatment) Regulations, which came into force on 1 October 2002. These latter regulations ensure that fixed-term employees receive no less favourable treatment than employees doing the same job who are employed on an open-ended basis. This applies to the ending of employment in the same way as it does to all other aspects and means that the same procedures used to dismiss an employee on an open-ended contract by reason of capability, conduct, redundancy and so on must also be used in relation to staff on fixed-term contracts. The example in Box 7.4 demonstrates the importance of consultation in relation to redundancy at the end of a fixed-term contract (see also the next section in relation to redundancy).

Redundancy

Consultation

The law requires that an employer who is intending to make 20 or more employees redundant in a period of less than 90 days must consult with recognized trade union representatives (or with other elected representatives of the workforce where no union is recognized). In many universities, particularly those that employ large

---

Box 7.4 Termination of fixed-term contracts – example[12]

Ms S had been employed on a succession of annual fixed-term contracts to teach English. In March 1999, she was asked to confirm her availability during the coming academic year and advised that she would be informed in April of the work that would be offered. In July 1999, she received an offer of work for the coming year which was 85 hours less than she had customarily worked. She was advised that she could either accept the offer and apply for additional work or accept redundancy. She claimed unfair dismissal. The EAT held that she had been unfairly dismissed as the first time she knew that she was at risk of redundancy was in July, and there had been no consultation with her.

---

numbers of staff on externally funded fixed-term contracts, it is not uncommon for in excess of 20 fixed-term contracts to expire and not be renewed in any 90-day period. While consultation with trade union representatives on the proposed redundancies will be the responsibility of the institution's personnel/HR professionals, dismissals by reason of redundancy have been found to be unfair when unions have been consulted but not individuals. ACAS recommends,[13] therefore, that it is best practice for individuals who are to be made redundant to be consulted as well. Line managers have an important part to play in this individual consultation by:

- ensuring that the staff affected are considered for suitable alternative work in the department;
- drawing to the attention of affected staff all vacancies within the department (and advising how to access information about vacancies elsewhere in the institution);
- keeping staff on externally funded fixed-term contracts informed of efforts to raise funds to extend their contracts;
- being aware of and applying for, if appropriate, any 'bridging funds' that may be available in the institution.

Right to time off to look for alternative work

An employee with two or more years' continuous service who is under notice of dismissal by reason of redundancy is entitled to reasonable time off, with pay, to look for alternative work. This will include staff employed on fixed-term contracts which are not to be renewed.

Statutory redundancy pay

An employee with two or more years' continuous service who is dismissed by reason of redundancy (including as a result of the non-renewal of a fixed-term contract) is entitled to a redundancy payment. The payment is calculated on the basis of the employee's age, length of service and the amount of a week's pay. The maximum payment is 30 weeks and there is a statutory limit on the maximum value of a week's pay[14] that may be used in the calculation (up-to-date information on the statutory limits on various payments may be found on the Department of Trade and Industry website). Line managers, particularly of externally funded research projects, should ensure that they are aware of the funding that is allocated by their institution for statutory redundancy payments.

Rights to notice and written reasons for dismissal

The law sets out minimum periods of notice that an employer must give an employee. These are set out in Table 7.1. The law requires employees who have been continuously employed for one month or more to give at least one week's notice. In practice, contractual notice periods, on both sides, for most staff with four or fewer years' service in a university or college, exceed the statutory minimum notice periods.

Most employees with at least one year's continuous service are entitled to receive, on request (either verbal or in writing), a written statement of the reasons for their dismissal or the non-renewal of their fixed-term contract. The employer must issue such a statement within 14 days of the request being made. An employee dismissed at any time during pregnancy or while on statutory maternity leave is

Table 7.1 Statutory notice periods

Length of continuous service	Minimum notice period
More than 1 month, but less than 2 years	No less than 1 week
2 years or more up to 12 years	No less than 2 weeks, plus: one additional week for each further completed year of service up to a maximum of 12 years
12 years or more	No less than 12 weeks

entitled to a written statement of the reasons for her dismissal, regardless of her length of service or whether she has requested one.

Wrongful dismissal

Failure to dismiss with notice, or with less than the period of notice specified in the contract, may give rise to a claim for damages for breach of contract due to wrongful dismissal. Some organizations include provision for pay in lieu of notice (Pilon) as an alternative to a notice period. While there are certain circumstances where dismissal without notice is justified (for example, summary dismissal for gross misconduct), it must be remembered that, if a contract includes a Pilon clause but does not explicitly state that gross misconduct will result in dismissal without notice or payment in lieu, then the employee will be contractually entitled to payment for the notice period (see also the following section in relation to the role of the visitor and the Model Statute).

Tenure and the Model Statute

The differences between the incorporated universities and colleges on the one hand, and the chartered universities on the other, with regard to the resolution of internal disputes are examined in Chapter 1. As a result of the judgement in the case of *Thomas* v. *University of Bradford*,[15] Section 206 of the Education Reform Act 1988 removed the exclusive jurisdiction of the visitor of a chartered university in relation to any dispute relating to the appointment or employment of a member of the academic staff, appointed or promoted after 20 November 1987, or the termination of such employment. The Act provided that any member of the academic staff appointed or promoted on or after 20 November 1987 would not have tenure, but could be dismissed by reason of redundancy. As the statutes governing the terms of academic appointments varied from one university to another, the Act provided that university commissioners would be appointed, empowered and required to make or amend charters, statutes, articles and so on in order to achieve the Act's principle objective. The commissioners' duties were not limited to ensuring that every institution to which the Act applied had provisions for dismissing academic staff by reason of redundancy and financial exigency. The Act also made provision for the introduction of disciplinary and grievance procedures for academic staff, and for appeal mechanisms to be put in place. The definition of 'good cause' was also to be extended so that a member of academic staff could be dismissed for failing to satisfactorily perform the duties of their post. The Model Statutes drafted by the commissioners for each qualifying institution were finally given Privy Council approval in late 1992/early 1993. In some instances, where universities already had provision in their statutes for the abolition of academic posts, the Model Statute imposed mechanisms which were more time-consuming than those which they replaced. Similarly, some universities had disciplinary and grievance procedures in place before the introduction of the Model Statute – these too were overtaken.

There were a number of difficulties with the original Model Statute. For example, it was unclear if it applied to the non-renewal of fixed-term contracts and to the dismissal of probationers; the procedures for redundancy and the dismissal of academic staff (as noted above) were cumbersome and there was ambiguity about the reasons for which academic staff might be dismissed. In January 2003, the Privy Council approved a draft revised Model Statute, drawn up by a working group under the auspices of Universities UK and the Universities and Colleges Employers Association, which was devised to address these difficulties. The draft revised Model Statute, which institutions could choose to incorporate into their own statutes (with Privy Council approval), introduced much simplified procedures, brought the reasons for dismissal of academic staff into line with those set out in the Employment Rights Act 1996 and clarified the position with regard to the non-confirmation of appointment at the end of the probationary period.

The Model Statute's provisions do not apply to the post-1992 universities or colleges of HE. Redundancy and dismissal procedures are required by the articles of government of their institutions and may be explicitly incorporated or implied in contracts of employment.

Academic freedom

There is no explicit protection in UK law.[16] However, the Education Reform Act required the university commissioners to be guided by certain principles when formulating changes to the chartered universities' rules, including: 'to ensure that academic staff have freedom within the law to question and test received wisdom, and to put forward new ideas and controversial or unpopular opinions, without placing themselves in jeopardy of losing their jobs or privileges they may have at their institutions'.[17]

This form of words was included verbatim as one of the three guiding principles by which the Model Statutes written for both

Loughborough University and the University of Leicester (and, no doubt, a great many others) are to be construed, so there is some contractual protection for academic freedom. However, the second of the other two guiding principles is: 'to enable the University to provide education, promote learning and engage in research *efficiently and economically*'.[18] This suggests that the use of published output (or lack of) as one of the selection criteria used to select academic staff for redundancy would not be necessarily an attack on academic freedom as is sometimes suggested, particularly if the university in question adheres to the third guiding principle: 'to apply the principles of justice and fairness'.

With rights come responsibilities. Academic freedom should not be used as a justification for personal criticism that goes beyond fair comment, inciting racial hatred or promoting discrimination, or otherwise infringing the rights of others. The University of Bath has adopted a code on *Academic Freedom and Corresponding Responsibilities* and this is reproduced in the Appendix to this chapter.

How to handle a dismissal fairly

Misconduct at work

Advice on fair disciplinary procedures may be found in Chapter 5, pages 114–121. Your personnel/HR department must be closely involved in any disciplinary process that could result in dismissal and will probably be responsible for formal communication with the member of staff and for note-taking. Also, the disciplinary procedure may well specify both the notice that must be given of meetings and the manner in which disciplinary hearings must be conducted. The importance of following the procedure fairly and consistently, even for minor offences, cannot be overemphasized – many employers have tribunal claims decided against them on procedural grounds alone. Therefore, the most important points are reiterated below.

Investigation

Your investigation should be fair, thorough and unbiased. Don't prejudge the value of evidence (for example, by interviewing only some witnesses). If you need to interview the member of staff, make it clear that it is as part of the investigation and not a disciplinary interview.

The disciplinary hearing

The member of staff should be invited in writing to the disciplinary hearing, with adequate notice, informing them of the reasons for the hearing and that they may be accompanied. Copies of statements or other evidence that is to be used should also be enclosed. The meeting should be postponed if either the member of staff, or their chosen companion, is unable to attend at the original time. (The law requires employees to make every effort to attend disciplinary meetings, so staff cannot demand an unreasonable postponement.) The meeting should be conducted in accordance with natural justice, ensuring, as far as possible, that the member of staff feels they have been given a fair hearing. Comprehensive (but not necessarily verbatim) notes must be taken and, if possible, the record of the meeting agreed by all parties.

If the member of staff lodges a grievance at any point in the disciplinary proceedings, either against their manager or regarding the manner in which the matter is being handled, the proceedings must be suspended while the grievance is dealt with.

The meeting should be adjourned while a decision is taken (otherwise it will appear that the outcome was prejudged before the member of staff had an opportunity to put their case). If it isn't possible to reconvene on the same day, a further meeting should be arranged, or the member of staff advised that they will be informed of the outcome in writing.

The outcome

The decision must be fair, consistent with practice in the organization and reasonable in all the circumstances. ACAS recommends that employers ask themselves the following questions if dismissal is contemplated:

- Is there sufficient reason for dismissal?
- Are there any reasonable alternatives to dismissal?
- Is dismissal consistent with the action taken in previous similar cases and with the disciplinary procedure?
- Would dismissal be fair, taking into account all the relevant factors?

The example in Box 7.5 demonstrates that even a dismissal for being asleep while on duty may be found to be unfair if it is not consistent with how other staff have been treated.

Even if it is decided that no further action should be taken, the member of staff should be advised of the outcome in writing and any

---

Box 7.5   Importance of consistency – example[19]

The employers condoned a relaxed regime at the weekends and employees could start and finish as they pleased, so long as the work was done. Sometimes the employees went home for lunch and sometimes they took naps while at work. One Sunday, Mr S was found asleep while at work. He was disciplined and dismissed. The dismissal was found to be unfair. The company had not demonstrated that he had failed to do his work, nor had it shown that, by falling asleep, he had put the plant at risk. Finally, the relaxed weekend regime was a material factor that should have been taken into account in determining a reasonable response.

---

warnings, even oral ones, should be noted down. It is important to remember that, if there is no record of warnings having been given in the past, the member of staff's past conduct should not be taken into account in determining the action to be taken as a result of formal disciplinary action. The case study in Box 7.6 illustrates the importance of documenting warnings.

The appeal

The member of staff should be notified of their right to appeal, and the procedure to follow if they wish to do so, in the letter confirming the outcome of the disciplinary hearing. Once again, your institution's formal disciplinary procedures will set out how the right to appeal may be exercised and who should consider an appeal.

Misconduct outside work

Misconduct does not have to take place at work to justify disciplinary action leading to dismissal. The ACAS *Code of Practice on Discipline and Grievance Procedures* advises that criminal charges or convictions outside employment should not be treated as automatic reasons for dismissal. If the conviction results in a long prison sentence, then the employment may end by the common law doctrine of frustration (meaning that it is no longer possible for the contract to be performed).[20] For other offences, the employer is required to consider all the relevant facts and decide whether the offence is sufficiently serious to warrant instituting the disciplinary procedure. The main consideration should be whether the offence is such that the member of staff is no longer suitable for the type of work for which they are employed.

Box 7.6   Case study – the importance of documenting warnings

Mrs O was a part-time cleaner who had worked for the university for more than 15 years. She had a reputation for being 'difficult' and had been transferred to different work stations on three separate occasions because of clashes with supervisory staff. Despite this, she had never been formally disciplined and there was no record of her even being spoken to about her conduct. While Mrs O was on paid sick leave from the university, her manager received an anonymous letter informing him that Mrs O was working for another employer. This was serious misconduct and, following an investigation in which it was confirmed that Mrs O had indeed been working elsewhere while on paid sick leave, she was invited to attend a disciplinary hearing. Mrs O admitted that she had just resumed work for her other employers (a part-time employment that her university managers were aware of and had not objected to) but that she was working in a desk-based supervisory capacity, not as a cleaner. She explained that she was able to undertake work that did not require any physical exertion but became breathless when cleaning, moving furniture, going up and down stairs and so on. The meeting was adjourned and her other employers contacted. They confirmed that Mrs O was working in solely in a supervisory capacity. Mrs O's managers still felt that her misconduct justified dismissal, particularly in the light of her behaviour over several years. However, it was strongly suspected that if she were to be dismissed she would lodge a claim for unfair dismissal with an employment tribunal and would present herself as a long-serving employee with a spotless disciplinary record who had been dismissed without warning for conduct that fell short of gross misconduct justifying summary dismissal. Mrs O's managers decided to issue her with a final written warning.

For example, if a member of the finance office were to be convicted of dishonesty, this would warrant disciplinary action up to and including dismissal. However, a conviction for dangerous driving would not necessarily justify an institution taking disciplinary action against an employee unless they were employed in a job which required them to drive.

Dismissal because of ill health

Chapter 5 (pages 101–102) considers long-term sickness absence, and the approaches that should be adopted where an eventual return to work is likely. However, there will be times when a return to work is impossible. The personnel/HR department should be closely involved in all such cases and will be responsible for liaising with the institution's medical advisers and communicating formally with the member of staff. Line managers should ensure that their colleagues in personnel/HR have up-to-date, accurate and comprehensive information about the member of staff's absence record, the nature of their job and the impact of their continued absence on the department's operations.

It is important that there is a review meeting, which may have to take place at the member of staff's home if they are not well enough to travel, to consult with the member of staff and inform them that the institution intends to seek medical advice. It may be the practice in your institution for line managers to accompany a representative of the personnel/HR department at such meetings. While the review meeting must be handled sensitively and sympathetically, it is necessary for the member of staff to be warned that they may be dismissed if, having taken advice, the conclusion is that they will be incapable of performing the job they were employed to do, either permanently or within a reasonable period. A dismissal may be judged unfair if the member of staff did not realize that dismissal was a possible outcome of the review process. The employee must consent to the employer having sight of a medical report produced either by their own GP or an independent doctor, but, if consent is withheld, the employer is entitled to make a decision on their future employment on the evidence that is available.

Once the report is received, a decision can be made taking into account not only the medical advice but also the impact of the member of staff's continued absence. If the report suggests that the member of staff may eventually be sufficiently recovered to return to work, a decision must be taken as to whether it is reasonable to continue holding the job open, and for how long. If the report suggests that, while they are not fit to undertake the job they were employed to do, but could undertake other work, the possibility of redeployment must be considered. This is particularly important for relatively large organizations such as universities and some of the larger colleges, as they are perceived to have the resources necessary to accommodate redeployment of this kind and failure to properly consider alternatives may lead to a dismissal being found to be unfair.

The management of short-term absences due to sickness was

examined in Chapter 5 (see pages 99–101). Where there is a poor sickness record and there is evidence of malingering, then it is appropriate to follow the disciplinary procedure and any resultant dismissal would be by reason of misconduct. However, if poor attendance is due to a variety of genuine, but apparently unrelated minor ailments, and there has been no improvement in a reasonable period of time, then it would be appropriate to follow the poor performance procedure outlined below. Ultimately, poor attendance due to unrelated sickness absences may provide grounds for dismissal for SOSR.

The Employment Act 2002 requires that an appeal mechanism is available to all dismissed employees, irrespective of the grounds for dismissal. While a dismissal as a result of long-term illness where medical evidence is not in dispute is unlikely to result in an appeal, dismissal on the grounds of a poor sickness absence record due to a variety of apparently unconnected minor ailments might well do.

Careful consideration must be given to whether the member of staff's illness may be classified as a disability under the DDA. See Chapter 5 (pages 102–104) for advice on what to do when a member of staff becomes disabled.

Dismissal because of poor performance

The crucial points to remember in relation to a dismissal for poor performance are:

- the member of staff must have been told what was expected of them;
- they must have been warned about their performance, and the consequences of failure to meet the required standard;
- they must have been given an opportunity to improve, together with necessary training.

Care must be taken to ensure that objective measures of performance are available so that undue reliance on subjective assessments can be avoided. It is also important to ensure that standards are applied consistently. As with dismissal on other grounds, an appeal mechanism must be available.

Handling resignations

Notice periods, and the person to whom a resignation should be addressed are usually specified in the relevant conditions of service. The notice period for academic and certain administrative staff in the chartered universities is often three months, to end on the last day of the month (although three calendar months and a term's notice are also common). In the incorporated universities, the notice period for academic staff is not uncommonly two months. For research and support staff, the notice period tends to be a month, while for most manual staff it is usually a week.

The conditions of service for research and support staff will normally state that resignations should be submitted to the head of department (although, in practice, research staff will often submit their resignation to their immediate line manager). It is important, therefore, that a standard procedure is adopted to ensure that the resignation, countersigned by the head of department, is forwarded to the personnel/HR department to ensure that the member of staff is removed from the payroll from the appropriate date. If the head of department has agreed to a shorter period of notice than that required by the conditions of service, this should be indicated.

Conditions of service vary with regard to how accrued holiday is treated when someone resigns. If the conditions of service require accrued holiday to be taken before the end of the notice period, or forfeited, then the member of staff should be reminded of this. However, if the conditions of service allow of payment in lieu of accrued holiday on the termination of the contract, then you should agree with the member of staff the amount of leave that will be outstanding at the end of the notice period and advise the payroll department in good time so that the necessary adjustment can be made to the final salary.

It is advisable for the line manager and the resigning member of staff to meet early in the notice period to agree a schedule of equipment, documents, computer files and so forth that belong to the institution and which must be surrendered by the end of the notice period. Depending on the job, the list could range from things as mundane as access cards, parking permits and keys to laptop computers, mobile phones and cars. For research posts, it is particularly important to resolve, as early as possible, any ambiguities regarding intellectual property rights and an agreed schedule for the delivery of outstanding work. A further meeting should be arranged on or close to the last working day to collect all outstanding items on the agreed list.

Exit questionnaires and interviews ■

Some institutions invite members of staff who are leaving to complete a confidential exit questionnaire, which is normally returned direct to the personnel/HR department. The information gathered from such questionnaires is usually aggregated to provide feedback on the reasons that employees have for leaving, their new employer (if they are changing jobs) and a forwarding address. One of the motivations for such questionnaires is that the Higher Education Statistics Agency requires information about the destination of academic and research staff who leave the institution. However, it can also provide useful information to support the development of staff retention strategies. Leaving staff may also be offered the option of a confidential exit interview with a representative of the personnel/HR department which may highlight problems in particular areas of the organization that should be addressed.

Employment references

Employers are not obliged to provide a reference for an employee (except, perhaps, because of a regulatory requirement, the employee is unable to get a job without one). However, in practice, it is very rare for an employer to refuse to provide a reference.[21] However, the employer owes a duty of care both to the subject of the reference and the recipient of it, and references must be:

- *Factually accurate*. In the case of *Spring* v. *Guardian Assurance Plc and Others*,[22] the House of Lords established that the employer owes a duty of care to employees and ex-employees to take reasonable care to ensure the accuracy of a reference. Mr S was an insurance salesman for Guardian Assurance. He was dismissed but was unable to find alternative work in the insurance sector because Guardian Assurance, which was required by the Life Assurance and Unit Trust Regulatory Organization rules to provide 'full and frank disclosure of all relevant matters which are believed to be true', provided a reference that described him as disloyal and unpopular and accused him of overselling to boost his commission. While the person who wrote the reference believed the contents to be true, they had not verified their statements, which a simple investigation would have shown to be untrue.
- *Fair and reasonable in all the circumstances*. In the case of *TSB Bank Plc* v. *Harris*,[23] providing a factually accurate reference was found not to be enough. Ms H had been employed by the bank for several years and had a chequered disciplinary record – in 1995, she received a final written warning for forgery when, to save time, she had initialled a document on behalf of a client. While that warning had expired, there were another 17 complaints made against her, but

because of the practice of the bank she was aware of only a few of these. When she had a job interview with another company, she disclosed the forgery matter. Her explanation was accepted and she was offered a job, subject to satisfactory references. When TSB provided a reference that outlined the complaints, but made no assessment of her work or character, the job offer was withdrawn. Ms H discovered what had happened, resigned and claimed constructive dismissal. The EAT found that the company had breached the implied duty of mutual trust and confidence in providing a reference which, while factually accurate, was neither fair nor reasonable.

In the case of *Cox* v. *Sun Alliance Life*,[24] the Court of Appeal suggested that an employer should refer to unresolved disciplinary proceedings and/or investigations only if the following requirements were met:

- the employer must genuinely believe the employee to be guilty of misconduct;
- there must be reasonable grounds for that belief;
- there must have been an adequate investigation into the matter.

Care must be taken to resist the temptation to provide a glowing reference for an employee dismissed for poor performance. In the cases of *Castledine* v. *Rothwell Engineering Ltd*[25] and *Haspell* v. *Rostron & Johnson Ltd*,[26] the employers were unable to sustain the argument that the dismissals were by reason of incompetence in the light of the favourable references that were provided in respect of the employees on leaving.

Since the enactment of the Data Protection Act 1998 and the issuing of the Employment Practices Data Protection Code, many organizations have adopted policies on who may provide references on their behalf. Before agreeing to provide a reference, you should familiarize yourself with your institution's policy.

Part 1 of the Employment Practices Data Protection Code states that confidential references are exempt from disclosure to the subject of the reference by the organization which gave it, but the exemption does not apply to the recipient. However, the recipient is entitled to withhold information that might identify the author of the reference. Increasingly, employers are adopting 'open reference' policies and stating that references will be released to the subject on request. Even where this is not the case, it is advisable to write a reference on the assumption that it might, at some time, be read by the subject.

Conclusion ■

While it would be preferable to part on good terms with all employees who leave the organization, we do not live in an ideal world. Mistakes will always be made, either by managers, when they select people (either out of optimism or desperation) for posts they are not really suited for, or by employees, who break the organization's rules. There will always be people whose work performance, in spite of reasonable support, fails to meet the required standard or who become so ill or disabled that they are unable to work. Hopefully, if the advice set out in earlier chapters of this book is followed, fewer infelicitous appointments will be made, and appropriate early intervention in tricky situations will minimize the number of cases which result in a dismissal. Where a parting of the ways on friendly terms is impossible, this chapter has, it is hoped, demonstrated that even these difficult cases can be resolved fairly.

Appendix ■

Automatically unfair grounds for dismissal

The Department of Trade and Industry list the following:

- pregnancy or any reason connected with maternity;
- taking, or seeking to take, parental leave or time off for dependants;
- taking certain specified types of health and safety action;
- refusing or proposing to refuse to do shop or betting work on a Sunday (England and Wales only);
- grounds related to rights under the Working Time Regulations 1998;
- performing or proposing to perform any duties relevant to an employee's role as an employee occupational pension scheme trustee or as a director of a trustee company;
- grounds related to acting as a representative for consultation about redundancy or business transfer, or as a candidate to be a representative of this kind, or taking part in the election of such a representative;
- making a protected disclosure within the meaning of the Public Interest Disclosure Act 1998;
- asserting a statutory employment right;
- grounds related to the national minimum wage;
- qualifying for working tax credit or seeking to enforce a right to it

(or because the employer was prosecuted or fined as a result of such action);
- trade union membership or activities, or non-membership of a trade union;
- taking lawfully organized official industrial action lasting eight weeks or less (or more than eight weeks, in certain circumstances);
- performing or proposing to perform any duties relating to an employee's role as a workforce representative or as a candidate to be such a representative for the purposes of the Transnational Information and Consultation of Employees Regulations 1999, or for taking, proposing to take or failing to take certain actions in connection with these regulations;
- grounds related to trade union recognition procedures;
- exercising or seeking to exercise the right to be accompanied at a disciplinary or grievance hearing, or to accompany a fellow worker;
- grounds related to the Part-time Workers (Prevention of Less Favourable Treatment) Regulations 2000;
- grounds related to the Fixed-term Employees (Prevention of Less Favourable Treatment) Regulations 2002.

University of Bath: *Academic Freedom and Corresponding Responsibilities*

Introduction
Academic freedom is necessary for the effective discharge of the duty of a university which, expressed in the words of the Charter, is 'to advance learning and knowledge by teaching and research' (Charter p. 2).

Over the centuries universities have had to struggle to establish, to maintain, and often to re-establish academic freedom, not for the comfort of academic staff, but for the health of the university. Where academic freedom has been suppressed the spirit of the university has suffered.

Like many qualities which are difficult to describe precisely, but which are nonetheless real (e.g. excellence, virtue), academic freedom is not easy to define. However, stimulated by the passing of the 1988 Education Reform Act, Academic Assembly set up a number of meetings which led to the formulation of the following code on *Academic Freedom and Corresponding Responsibilities*. After acceptance by Academic Assembly, it was approved by Senate on 2 November 1988, and subsequently by Council.

The institution

Freedom
To govern its own affairs, in particular, in teaching and research.

Corresponding responsibility
To maintain academic standards and independence of judgement.

Members of the university

Freedom
Within the law to question and test received wisdom and to put forward new ideas and controversial or unpopular opinions.

Corresponding responsibility
To support the same freedoms for those of differing views.

Freedom
To discuss the university's affairs, in appropriate media.

Corresponding responsibility
To enter into such discussion with integrity and charity, not representing personal opinions as those of the university.

Academic staff

Freedom
To take an active part in the governance of the university.

Corresponding responsibility
To accept decisions properly arrived at.

Freedom
To select methods of teaching course elements which have been properly agreed.

Corresponding responsibility
To take full cognizance of (i) the intellectual and professional needs of students and (ii) the requirement for the integrity and coherence of an academic course.

Freedom
To select one's area of research, subject to constraints on the resources available; to publish subject to academic judgement.

Corresponding responsibility
To maintain high standards of scholarship and to be responsive to reasoned discussion.

Freedom
Not to take part in research which is morally repugnant to the individual.

Corresponding responsibility
Not to use such freedom in a fickle way.

NOTES

∎

Chapter 1

1 In Scotland, there were the four 'ancient' universities of St Andrews, Glasgow, Aberdeen and Edinburgh, all created between 1413 and 1583.
2 Lowe, R. (1983) The expansion of higher education in England, in K.H. Jarausch (ed.) *The Transformation of Higher Learning 1860–1930*. Chicago: University of Chicago Press.
3 Chelsea was incorporated into the University of London.
4 Cobban, A. (1988) *The Medieval Universities: Oxford and Cambridge to c1500*. Aldershot: Scolar Press.
5 Bridge, J.W. (1970) Keeping the peace in the universities: the role of the visitor, *Law Quarterly Review*, 86: 531–51.
6 *Thomas* v. *University of Bradford* [1987] 1 All ER 834.
7 Cobban, A. (1988) op. cit. p. 99.
8 Raelin, J.A. (1985) *The Clash of Cultures: Managers Managing Professionals*. Boston, MA: Harvard Business School Press.
9 Partington, P. (1994) *Human resources management and development in higher education*, paper presented to the Quinquennial Conference of the Conference of European Rectors, Budapest.
10 MacKay, I. (1995) The personnel function in the universities of northern England, *Personnel Review*, 24(7): 41–53.

Chapter 2

1 *Biggs* v. *Bcs Services Ltd.* (unreported, ET Case No. 3200996/99 D7233).
2 *Mallidi* v. *The Post Office* (unreported, ET Case No. 2403719/1998).
3 *Sunner and others* v. (1) *Air Canada* and (2) *Alpha Catering Services*, Case Nos. 2303121/97 and others. Reported in *EOR Discrimination Case Law Digest*, 36, 1998.

4 *Arshad* v. *Council of the City of Newcastle-upon-Tyne*, Case No. 8314/89. Reported in *EOR Discrimination Case Law Digest*, 4, 1990.

5 *Farnsworth* v. (1) *London Borough of Hammersmith and Fulham* and (2) *Cooper* (unreported, ET Case No. 2201799/98).

6 *Tyrell* v. *British Airways plc* (unreported, ET Case No. 2300931/99).

7 *McCaull* v. *British Gas Services* (unreported, ET Case No. 2304918/97).

8 *Kohnstam* v. *Middlesborough Borough Council* (unreported, ET Case No. 2500362/98).

9 NACRO for the Forum on the Employment of Ex-Offenders in Care Settings (2001) *Recruiting Safely: Guidance for Employers and Other Bodies in the Health and Social Care Field on Recruiting and Retaining Staff and Volunteers with Criminal Records*. London: NACRO.

10 Service under a fixed-term contract before 1 October 2002 will not count. This means the practical effects of this aspect of the regulations will not be seen until the latter part of 2006.

11 Robertson, I.T. and Smith, M. (2001) Personnel selection, *Journal of Occupational and Organizational Psychology*, 74(4): 441–72.

12 *Stapp* v. *The London Borough of Hillingdon* (unreported, ET Case No. 32787/ 78).

13 *Faris* v. *Red Cross* (unreported, COET 3736/90).

Chapter 3 ■

1 The Institute of Personnel and Development (1997) *Labour Turnover Survey* indicated that almost a quarter of leavers had less than six months' service.

2 *The Post Office* v. *Mughal* [1977] IRLR 178, EAT.

3 *Patey* v. *Taylor and Wishart* [1988] IRLIB 350, EAT.

4 *National Agreement Concerning the Procedure and Criteria to be Used in Connection with the Probation Period for Non-Clinical Academic Staff*, 1974.

5 DfES (Department for Education and Skills) (2003) *The Future of Higher Education*, Cm 5735. London: HMSO.

6 RCI (Research Careers Initiative) (1998) *Employing Contract Researchers: A Guide to Best Practice*. http://www.universitiesuk.ac.uk/activities/RCI-downloads/RCIContractResearchers.pdf (accessed 1 September 2003).

7 CIPD (Chartered Institute of Personnel and Development) (1999, updated September 2002) *On-the-job Training* (Quick Fact), http://www.cipd.co.uk/infosource/Training/On-the-job-training.asp (accessed 23 June 2003).

Chapter 4 ■

1 Pugh, D. (1983) *Writers on Organizations*, 3rd edn. Harmondsworth: Penguin.

2 Deem, R., Fulton, O, Read, M. and Watson, S. (2001) *'New Managerialism' and the Management of UK Universities*, End of Award Report. Swindon, Economic and Social Research Council (http://www.regard.ac.uk/regard/home/index_html)

3 Newman, F. and Couturier, L. (2002) *Trading Public Good in the Higher Education Market.* London: Observatory on Borderless Higher Education, Association of Commonwealth Universities (http.//www.obhe.ac.uk).

4 (i) CVCP (2000) (now Universities UK) *The Business of Borderless Education: UK Perspectives.* London: CVCP. (ii) Cunningham, S., Tapsall, S., Ryan, Y. *et al.* (1998) *New Media and Borderless Education: A Review of the Convergence Between Global Media Networks and Higher Education Provision,* 97/22. Canberra: Department of Employment, Education, Training and Youth Affairs. (iii) Cunningham, S., Ryan, Y. *et al.* (2000) *The Business of Borderless Education,* 00/3. Canberra: Department of Education, Training and Youth Affairs.

5 Department for Education and Skills (DfES) (2003) *The Future of Higher Education.* London: HMSO.

6 Ibid.

7 Ibid.

8 Davies, J. (1998) *The Dialogue of Universities with their Stakeholders: Comparisons Between Different Regions of Europe.* Geneva: Council of European Rectors (now European Universities Association).

9 Performance and Innovation Unit (now Cabinet Office Strategy Unit) (2001) *Strengthening Leadership in the Public Sector,* www.cabinet-office.gov.uk/innovation/zip/default.htm, accessed 4 April 2001.

10 Confederation for British Industry/Trades Union Congress (2001) *The UK Productivity Challenge.* London: CBI/TUC.

11 Council for Excellence in Management and Leadership (CEML) (2002) *Managers and Leaders: Raising Our Game.* London: CEML.

12 Brumbrach, G. (1998) Some ideas, issues and predictions about performance management, *Public Personnel Management,* winter: 381–402.

13 Armstrong, M. (2002) *The Performance Management Audit,* p. 5. Cambridge: Cambridge Strategy Publications Ltd.

14 Ibid.

15 Performance Management in the UK: Analysis of the Issues. Institute of Personnel Management (1992). London, CIPD.

16 Ashridge Management College (2002) *Performance Management,* www.ashridge.intereliant.com/ASHRIDGE/vavlrc.nst/site/PEMLG02.hbu, accessed 30 November 2002.

17 Guest, D. (1998) Combine harvest, *People Management,* 25 October: 64–6.

18 Armstrong, M. (2000) *Performance Management: Key Strategies and Practical Guidelines,* 2nd edn. London: Kogan Page.

19 IRS (1996) Using human resources to achieve strategic objectives, *IRS Management Review,* July: 21–32.

20 Winstanley, D. and Stuart-Smith, K. (1996) Policing performance: the ethics of performance management, *Personnel Review,* 25 (6): 66–84.

21 Taylor, F. (1911) *The Principles of Scientific Management.* New York. Harper & Row.

22 Wheatley, M. (1994) *Leadership and the New Science: Learning about Organizations from an Orderly Universe.* San Francisco: Berrett-Koehler Publishers.

23 Lyotard, J-F. (1984) *The Postmodern Condition: A Report on Knowledge.* Manchester: Manchester University Press.

24 Jones, P. (2002) Performance management: surviving the sea of change, Innovations in executive and organisational development, 2002. (pp. 16–21) Berkhampstead, Ashridge (http://www.ashridge.com/innovations)

25 Handy, C. (1985) *Understanding Organisations*, 3rd edn. Harmondsworth: Penguin.

26 Jones, P. (2002) op. cit.

27 Buckingham, M. and Coffman, C. (1999) *First Break all the Rules*. New York: Simon & Schuster.

28 Crane, M. (2002) Winning hearts and minds: leadership and performance management, www.ncsl.org.uk, accessed 1 December 2002.

29 Middlehurst, R. and Garrett, R. (2001) *Developing Senior Managers: Summary Report*. Sheffield: Higher Education Staff Development Agency.

30 Manzoni, J-F. and Barsoux, J-L. (1998) The set-up-to-fail syndrome, *Harvard Business Review*, March–April: 101–13.

31 Manzoni, J-F. (2002) A better way to deliver bad news, *Harvard Business Review*, September: 114–19.

32 For example, Armstrong, M. (2002) op. cit.

33 Quoted in Handy, C. (1994) *The Empty Raincoat*. London: Arrow Books.

Chapter 5 ▮

1 CIPD (2002) *Employee Absence 2002: A Survey of Management Policy and Practice*. London: CIPD.

2 Factors costed in included occupational and statutory sick pay, replacement labour costs, overtime and reduced performance.

3 *IRS Employment Review* (2002) 758 (19 August): 44.

4 TUC (Trades Union Congress) (2001) *Creating a Healthier Nation: Getting Britain Back to Work*. London: TUC.

5 Fisher Meredith Solicitors (2002) *Employment Law Newsletter*, June. www.fishermeredith.co.uk/emplaw_news.html, accessed 2 February 2003.

6 *IRS Employment Review* (2002) 758 (19 August): 9.

7 Including Essex, Kent, Loughborough, Nottingham and Warwick.

8 Alcohol is estimated to be the cause of 3–5 per cent of all absences from work (about 8–14 million working days a year). See Holtermann, S. and Burchell, A. (1981) *Government Economic Service Working Party*, No. 37. London: DHSS.

9 Alcohol from two pints of normal strength beer (or half a bottle of wine) consumed at lunchtime will still be present in the blood three hours later; heavy drinking in the evening may mean that the concentration of alcohol in the bloodstream the following morning is in excess of the legal drink-drive limit. See HSE (1996) *Don't Mix It! – A Guide for Employers on Alcohol at Work*. London: HSE UK.

10 Ibid.

11 That is, those covered by the Misuse of Drugs Act 1971.

12 Source: alcohol and drugs policy of the University of Warwick.

13 *Goodwin* v. *The Patent Office* [1999] IRLR 4, EAT.

14 *Young* v. *The Post Office* [2002] IRLR 660, CA.

15 HSE website: http://www.hse.gov.uk/stress/index.htm, accessed 2 February 2003.

16 *Walker* v. *Northumberland County Council* [1995] 1 All ER 737, QBD.

17 At the time of writing, a draft equality bill had been published covering discrimination in employment on the grounds of sex, race, disability, marital or family status, sexual orientation and age. As well as proposing a single equality commission, it also extended the positive duty requirement of the Race Relations (Amendment) Act to sex and disability.

18 CIPD (issued May 1997, revised March 2002) *Harassment at Work* (Quick Fact).   http://www.cipd.co.uk/infosource/EqualityandDiversity/Harassment.asp, accessed 30 November 2002.

19 Hammond, D. (2001) Someone to lean on, *People Management*, 7(24): 33–7.

20 Hoel, H. and Cooper, C.L. (2000) *Destructive Conflict and Bullying at Work*. Manchester: Manchester School of Management.

21 Source: Loughborough University policy on harassment and bullying.

Chapter 6

1 The author has drawn on the following sources in the preparation of this chapter: Stredwick, J. and Ellis, S. (1998) *Flexible Working Practices (Techniques and Innovations)*. Institute of Personnel and Development London, CIPD; University of Bradford (2002) *Teleworking at BT – The Environmental and Social Impacts of its Workabout Scheme*. Bradford: University of Bradford and the UK Centre for Economic and Environmental Development; Weightman, J. (1999) *Managing People*. Institute of Personnel and Development London, CIPD; *People Management* (2002) *The Guide to Work-life Balance*, September Supplement.

2 Kodz, J. *et al.* (2002) *Working Hours in the UK*. Employment Relations Research Series Number 16. London: DTI. http://www.dti.gov.uk/er/emar/longhours.htm accessed 1 September 2003.

3 DTI/*Management Today* (2002) *Management Today*, September.

4 University of Bradford (2002) *Teleworking at BT – The Environmental and Social Impacts of its Workabout Scheme*. Bradford: University of Bradford and the UK Centre for Economic and Environmental Development.

5 Northern Rock benefits from work-life balance workshops. Higginbottom, K. (2002) *People Management*, 24 October. http://www.peoplemanagement.co.uk/archiveitem.asp?id=7862, accessed 2 September 2003.

6 A report produced by the Association of Graduate Recruiters in 1999, *Should I Stay or Should I Go?*, indicated that graduates in their first jobs want to 'work to live' rather than 'live to work' and to achieve a better balance between their work and home lives than their parents did.

7 University of Central Lancashire, Leeds Metropolitan University, Middlesex University, Oxford Brookes University and Trinity College, Dublin.

8 Previously known as industrial tribunals.

9 Some of the text used in this section is adapted from the DTI website (www.dti.gov.uk), which provides an excellent source of information for employers.

10 Statutory maternity pay is earnings related, paid by the employer on behalf of the government. Women who are ineligible for statutory maternity pay may be eligible for maternity allowance and they should contact their local social security office as soon as possible after the twenty-sixth week of pregnancy.

11 *Marshall* v. *Devon County Council* [2000] (unreported ET Case No. 1701005/00).

12 An internal work-life balance survey conducted by IBM in 2001 revealed that difficulties in balancing workloads and caring responsibilities were leading to employees leaving the organization.

13 *Wright* v. *Rugby Borough Council* [1984] (unreported ET Case No. 23528/84).

14 *Lockwood* v. *Crawley Warren Group Ltd* [2000] IRLB 654, EAT.

15 DTI/*Management Today* (2002) op. cit.

Chapter 7

1 Farrington, D.J. (1998) *The Law of Higher Education*, 2nd edn, p. 463. London: Butterworths.

2 Although there is no service requirement in relation to a number of 'automatically unfair grounds', which are set out in the Appendix to this chapter (see pages 177–178).

3 *Lovie* v. *Anderson* [1999] IRLR 164, EAT.

4 *Medway Community Living Services* v. *Poole* [2000] IRLB 638, EAT.

5 *Williams and Other* v. *Whitbread Company Ltd* [1996] CA, 19 June.

6 *Tesco Stores* v. *Othman-Khalid* [2002] IDS 703, EAT.

7 See also Chapter 2, pages 18–19.

8 *3rd (Interim) Report*, RCI, September 2001.

9 *Morrow* v. *Safeway Stores* [2001] IDS Brief 699, EAT.

10 *Abbey National* v. *Robinson* [2001] IDS Brief 680, EAT.

11 *Ball* v. *La Retraite Roman Catholic Girls School Governors* [2002] ELR 125, EAT.

12 *Stankovic* v. *City of Westminster* [2001] IDS Brief 699, EAT.

13 ACAS (2002) *Redundancy Handling*. Online publication, http://www.acas.org.uk/publications/B08.html (accessed 23 June 2003).

14 From 1 February 2003 the rate was £260.

15 *Thomas* v. *University of Bradford* [1987] 1 All ER 834.

16 It is possible that the Human Rights Act 2000, which gives effect to Article 8 of the European Convention on Human Rights (the right to freedom of expression) offers protection for academic freedom. However, at the time of writing, this had not been tested.

17 Education Reform Act 1988 s202 (2)(a).

18 Author's emphasis.

19 *William Grant and Sons (Distillers) Ltd* v. *Stuart* [1999] IRLR 609, CSIH.

20 See Mordue, C. in D. Palfreyman and D. Warner (eds) (2002) *Higher Education Law* (Bristol: Jordan's) p. 220 for a discussion of the doctrine of frustration.

21 Tribunals have found that a refusal to provide a reference can be discriminatory. For example, in the case of (i) *Coote* v. *Granada Hospitality 2* (1999

IRLR 452, EAT), Coote was awarded £190,000 in compensation for sex discrimination when refused a reference and (ii) in *Chief Constable of West Yorkshire Police* v. *Khan* (2001 IRLR 830, CA), Khan was awarded £1500 for injury to feelings when the refusal to provide a reference was found to be racial discrimination.

22 *Spring* v. *Guardian Assurance Plc and Others* [1994] IRLR 460, HL.
23 *TSB Bank Plc* v. *Harris* [2000] IRLR 157, EAT.
24 *Cox* v. *Sun Alliance Life* [2001] EWCA Civ 649, CA.
25 *Castledine* v. *Rothwell Engineering Ltd* [1973] IRLR 99.
26 *Haspell* v. *Rostron & Johnson Ltd* [1976] IRLR 50.

FURTHER READING AND
USEFUL WEBSITES

Chapter 1

Further reading

Warner, D. and Palfreyman, D. (eds) (2001) *The State of UK Higher Education*. Buckingham: Open University Press.

Chapter 2

Further reading

Commission for Racial Equality (CRE) (1984) *Code of Practice: For the Elimination of Racial Discrimination and the Promotion of Equality of Opportunity in Employment*. London: CRE.

Commission for Racial Equality (CRE) (1997) *Racial Equality and the Asylum and Immigration Act 1996: A Guide for Employers on Compliance with the Race Relations Act 1976*. London: CRE.

Disability Rights Commission (DRC) (1996) *The Disability Discrimination Act 1995: What Employers Need To Know*. Stratford-upon-Avon: DRC.

Disability Rights Commission (DRC) (1999) *Employing Disabled People: A Good Practice Guide for Managers and Employers*. Stratford-upon-Avon: DRC.

Chapter 3

Further reading

Partington, P. and Stainton C. (2002) *Managing Staff Development*. Buckingham: Open University Press.

Chapter 5

Further reading
UCEA (1999) *A Guide to Dealing with Stress in HE*. London: UCEA.
Edworthy, A. (2000) *Managing Stress*. Buckingham: Open University Press.
Health and Safety Executive (HSE) (2001) *Tackling Work-related Stress: A Manager's Guide to Improving and Maintaining Employee Health and Well-being*. London: HSE.

Websites
Bullying
Bully online (http://www.successunlimited.co.uk/bully/index.htm).

Discipline and grievances
ACAS (www.acas.gov.uk).

Harassment
Equal Opportunities Commission (www.eoc.org.uk).
Commission for Racial Equality (www.cre.gov.uk).
Disability Rights Commission (www.drc-gb.org.uk).

Stress
UK Workstress Network (http://www.workstress.net/).

Chapter 6

Websites
www.diversity-whatworks.gov.uk/workbalance.htm.
www.dti.gov.uk/work-lifebalance
www.employersforwork-lifebalance.org.uk
www.familyfriendly.com
www.flexibility.co.uk
www.homeworking.com
www.peoplemanagement.co.uk/work-life
www.unison.org.uk
www.workingfromhome.co.uk
www.worklifebalance.com

Chapter 7

Further reading
Academic freedom and the Model Statute
Palfreyman, D. and Warner, D. (eds) (2002) *Higher Education Law*, 2nd edn Bristol: Jordans.

Website
Department of Trade and Industry Employment Relations Directorate (www.dti.gov.uk/er).

INDEX

MANAGING STAFF DEVELOPMENT

Patricia Partington and Caroline Stainton

Managing Staff Development is a handbook to help university and college managers in their planning, delivery and evaluation of staff development. It is distinctive in its coverage of development for all functions in higher education: educational development, management training and professional training for all groups of staff including administrators, technicians, managers, researchers and tutors. It focuses on the manager's role and responsibilities in respect of all staff (rather than on a particular group or function) and concentrates on the full cycle of planning, execution and review of staff development to ensure its benefits for both individuals and the institutions. It is a practical guide that includes working examples of programmes and activities and covers the entire range of staff development from individual personal development through departmental and faculty-based activities to national developments and examples.

Managing Staff Development is an invaluable resource for heads of department, senior managers, directors of central services, and staff responsible for managing personal and professional development within universities and colleges.

Contents
Staff development: what is it and how has it evolved? – The manager's role in and responsibilities for staff development – The organization of staff development in departments – Managing staff development for learning and teaching – Managing staff development for research and scholarship – Managing staff development for leadership, management and administration – Managing staff development for the use of new technology – Achieving a holistic and integrated approach to staff development – Evaluating staff development and harnessing its potential – References – Index.

256pp   0 335 20957 2 (Paperback)   0 335 20958 0 (Hardback)

DEPARTMENTAL LEADERSHIP IN HIGHER EDUCATION
Peter T. Knight and Paul R. Trowler

This book is primarily aimed at those who have, or will have, a role in leading departments or teams in higher education institutions. It examines the ways in which mainstream leadership thinking does – and does not – apply to departments and teams in HEIs and suggests that departmental leadership is critical to institutional well-being. A series of substantive chapters explores assessment, learning and teaching, research and scholarship, administration and continuing professional development, and the final chapter discusses the ways in which individuals learn how to lead. The book offers a way of looking at the practice of leading rather than presenting a selection of tips or tools for leadership, but is studded with fascinating views from departmental leaders and extensive practical advice.

Contents

Preface – Contexts – Changing – Leadership theory, leadership practice – Leading in higher education departments – Learning from other places – Issues – Leading and assessment – Leading learning and teaching – Leading research and scholarship – Administration and positioning – Continuing professional development – Learning to lead – Conclusion – References – Index.

224pp   0 335 20675 1 (Paperback)   0 335 20676 X (Hardback)